for my sister
Deborah
Best friends forever
♡

GIRL'S GUIDE
TO FUN & FUNKY KNITTING

from tops to flip-flops

KATHLEEN GRECO
& NICK GRECO

C&T PUBLISHING

Copyright © 2006 by Dimensional Illustrators, Inc.

Published by C&T Publishing, Inc., P.O. Box 1456, Lafayette, CA, 94549; and Dimensional Illustrators, Inc., 362 Second Street Pike #112, Southampton, PA, 18966, Phone: (215) 953-1415 Email: jellyyarn@3dimillus.com, Website: www.jellyyarn.com

Front cover: Boat Neck Top, Tankini Top
Back cover: Beaded Flip-Flops, Bell Sleeved Sweater, Boa Scarf

Knitwear Designs, Artwork and Text Copyright © 2006 by Dimensional Illustrators, Inc.

Attention Teachers: C&T Publishing, Inc. encourages you to use this book as a text for teaching. Contact us at 800-284-1114 or www.ctpub.com for more information about the C&T Teachers Program.

We take great care to ensure that the information included in our books is accurate and presented in good faith, but no warranty is provided nor results guaranteed. Having no control over the choices of materials or procedures used, neither the author nor C&T Publishing, Inc., shall have any liability to any person or entity with respect to any loss or damage caused directly or indirectly by the information contained in this book. For your convenience, we post an up-to-date listing of corrections on our website (www.ctpub.com). If a correction is not already noted, please contact our customer service department at ctinfo@ctpub.com or at P.O. Box 1456, Lafayette, CA, 94549.

Trademark (™) and registered trademark (®) names are used throughout this book. Rather than use the symbols with every occurrence of a trademark or registered trademark name, we are using the names only in the editorial fashion and to the benefit of the owner, with no intention of infringement.

Library of Congress Cataloging-in-Publication Data

Greco, Kathleen.
  Girl's guide to fun & funky knitting : from tops to flip-flops / Kathleen
Greco & Nick Greco.
    p. cm.
  Includes index.
  ISBN-13: 978-1-57120-382-3 (paper trade)
  ISBN-10: 1-57120-382-6 (paper trade)
  1. Knitting--Juvenile literature. 2. Knitting--Patterns--Juvenile literature.
  I. Greco, Nick. II. Title. III. Title: Girl's guide to fun and funky knitting.
  TT820.G824 2006
  746.43'2--dc22
                      2006008182

ISBN 10: 1-57120-382-6
ISBN 13: 978-1-57120-382-3

Printed in China 10 9 8 7 6 5 4 3 2 1

Publisher **Amy Marson**

Editorial Director **Gailen Runge**

Acquisitions Editor **Jan Grigsby**

Creative Director / Creative Editor **Kathleen Greco** *Dimensional Illustrators, Inc.*

Executive Editor **Nick Greco** *Dimensional Illustrators, Inc.*

Book Design and Typography **Deborah Davis** *Deborah Davis Design*

Knitwear Designs **Kathleen Greco** *Dimensional Illustrators, Inc.*

Fashion Photographer **Joe VanDeHatert** *Studio V*

Knitting and Yarn Photography **Kathleen Greco** *Dimensional Illustrators, Inc.*

Knitter Girl Illustrator **Catherine Davis** *Catherine Davis Art and Design*

Knitting Consultants **Karen Greenwald** and **Maria Williams**

Knitters **Lisa Gibson** and **Christen Parzych**

Acknowledgments
We wish to thank our talented models Meghan, Hannah, Olivia, Chloé, and their wonderful parents for their hard work and cooperation during the production of this book. A special thank you to Deborah for her graphic design and Catherine for her cool knitter girl illustrations. Thanks to Joe VanDeHatert for his exciting fashion photographs, and Wendy for her assistance and support. All our love to our dear friends and family.

–Nick and Kathleen

CONTENTS

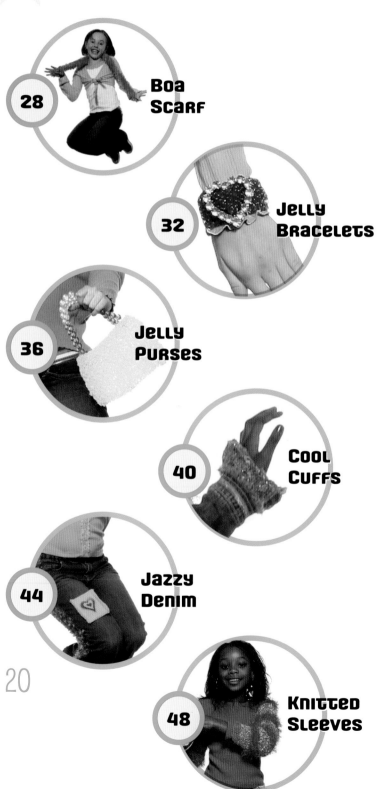

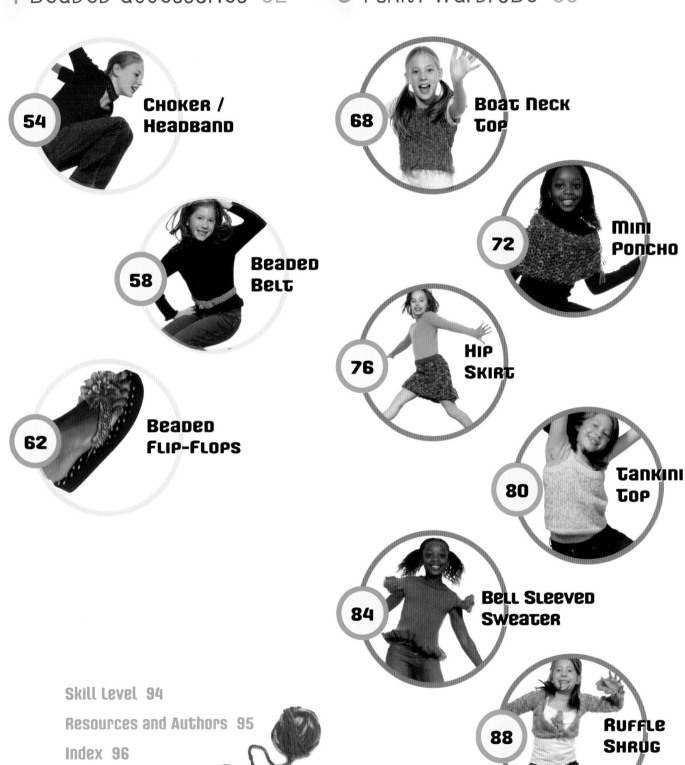

INTRODUCTION

GIRL'S GUIDE
TO FUN & FUNKY KNITTING

features 15 cool fashions and fun accessories for you to knit.
Patterns are designed for girls ages eight to fourteen, with sizes
small to extra-large. The project patterns are made for all skill
levels: Easy, for the first time knitter (Garter Stitch only); Beginner,
for those who know how to Knit and Purl (Garter and Stockinette
Stitch); Advanced Beginner, for those who know how to Knit,
Purl, Increase and Decrease, (Garter Stitch and Stockinette Stitch
with a little shaping). Each pattern lists the needles, yarn, and
materials needed for each project. If you don't find the yarn listed,
look in the Substitution Yarn list next to the pattern.

Chapter 1 teaches you how-to knit with lotsa' easy-to-follow
photographs. Even if you've never picked up knitting needles
before, don't worry, we'll teach you the basics, from casting on to
binding off and we'll show you how to read a knitting pattern.

Chapter 2 explores the variety of novelty yarns with fun symbols including—eyelash, fur, fuzz, ribbon, and jelly yarns. Learn tricks about working with yarn and helpful "knitting trouble" tips.

In chapter 3, learn to knit easy, fun stuff and embellishments. Knit a fluffy boa scarf in fab fun colors, and make mod jelly bracelets and purses. Personalize your jeans with knit and rubber stamped patches and pockets, and spice up boring sweaters with sassy sleeves and cuffs.

Beads are the must-have fashion accessory. In chapter 4, knit a cool choker or headband with metallic pony beads, make a hip beaded belt, and add zing to flip-flops with glass beads and *Jelly Yarn*.

In chapter 5, begin creating your own funky wardrobe. Start with a simple boat neck top design, continue with a mini poncho and hip skirt, welcome spring with a cool tankini top, and finish with a fashionable bell sleeved sweater and ruffle shrug.

Follow our knitter girl throughout the book. She'll be your best girlfriend for tips on hassle-free, fun knitting! So, if U R ready to go

LET'S START KNITTING!

1 LEARN TO KNIT

Slipknot and Long Tail Cast On

Jump-start your knitting experience with a simple Slipknot and Long Tail Cast On. You're on your way to knitting mania!

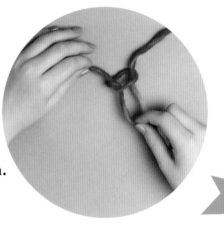

Knit Stitch

Master the Garter stitch pattern by learning this basic Knit stitch. Guaranteed to be your fave stitch. Let's start knitting scarves, bracelets and purses!

Purl Stitch

Once you learn this, combine knit and purl stitches for a hot Stockinette stitch pattern. Start knitting some kool tops, skirts, and shrugs!

Easy Increasing and Easy Decreasing

Get your outfits in superb shape with some simple skills that will give your knitted outfits a funky look and great fit.

Binding Off

To keep your wonderful knitted work from unraveling, you must bind off. Follow 3 simple steps, and you'll have a perfect ending.

Sewing It All Together

It's fun to see all the knitted pieces come together. The Mattress stitch is easy to do and makes a nearly invisible seam. Weave in the loose ends, block it, and party with your favorite friends.

Slipknot

Begin a knitting project with a simple slipknot. The slipknot is the first cast on stitch in the pattern.

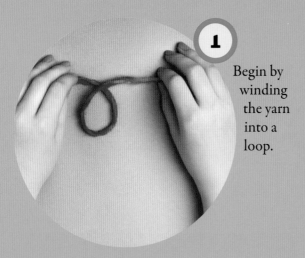

1 Begin by winding the yarn into a loop.

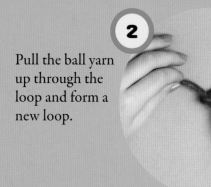

2 Pull the ball yarn up through the loop and form a new loop.

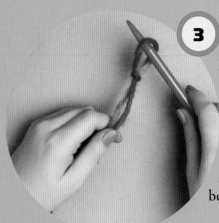

3 Place the loop on the needle and tighten. Make the knot snug but not too tight. You are now ready to begin casting on.

Long Tail Cast On

To begin knitting, you must cast on the required number of stitches called for in the pattern. This cast on technique is one of the easiest methods for beginning a knitting project.

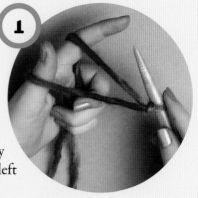

1 Form a slingshot with the tail yarn wrapped around your thumb and index fingers. Hold both strands securely in the palm of your left hand.

2 Place the needle point under the yarn on your thumb and lift from the bottom up.

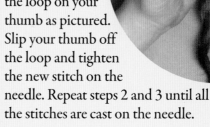

3 Insert the needle behind the yarn on your index finger. Draw the needle through the loop on your thumb as pictured. Slip your thumb off the loop and tighten the new stitch on the needle. Repeat steps 2 and 3 until all the stitches are cast on the needle.

Knit Stitch

The Knit stitch is the first basic stitch in knitting. With a Knit stitch, keep the ball of yarn in back of the needles. Knitting every row will create a basic Garter stitch fabric. The abbreviation for the Knit stitch is K.

1 Insert the right-hand needle from left to right (knitwise) into the first cast on stitch. As you work each stitch, slide the remaining stitches to the tip of the needle. Form an X with the right-hand needle below the left-hand needle.

2 Wind the yarn counterclockwise around the right-hand needle and pull the yarn down between the needles. When working a Knit stitch, make sure the ball of yarn is in back.

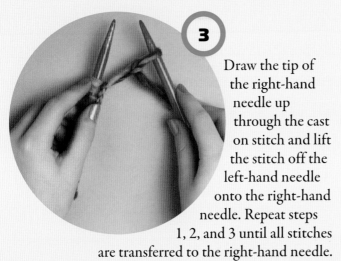

3 Draw the tip of the right-hand needle up through the cast on stitch and lift the stitch off the left-hand needle onto the right-hand needle. Repeat steps 1, 2, and 3 until all stitches are transferred to the right-hand needle.

Purl Stitch

The Purl stitch is the second basic stitch in knitting. With a Purl stitch, keep the ball of yarn in front of the needles. Knitting 1 row and purling 1 row will create a basic Stockinette stitch fabric. The abbreviation for the Purl stitch is P.

1 Insert the right-hand needle from right to left (purlwise) into the next stitch. When purling, always keep the ball of yarn in front.

2 Wrap the yarn counterclockwise around the tip of the right-hand needle.

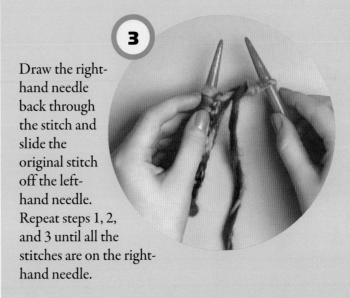

3 Draw the right-hand needle back through the stitch and slide the original stitch off the left-hand needle. Repeat steps 1, 2, and 3 until all the stitches are on the right-hand needle.

Easy Increase

To make your knitwear wider, you will need to increase the number of stitches. This is a simple technique to widen what you are knitting. By knitting into the front and back of the same stitch, you will create 2 stitches from 1 original stitch. The abbreviation for increasing is Inc.

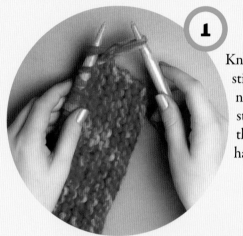

1 Knit one stitch but do not slip the stitch off the left-hand needle.

2 Insert the tip of the right-hand needle into the back of the same stitch, wrap the yarn counter-clockwise and knit as usual.

3 Slip the stitch off the left-hand needle. You have created 2 stitches from the original stitch and completed an easy increase.

Easy Decrease

You will need to decrease stitches to shape your knitwear. Knitting 2 stitches together is a simple technique for slanting your knitwear to the right. The abbreviation for knitting 2 stitches together is K2tog.

Right-Slanting

1 Insert the tip of the needle knitwise into the next 2 stitches together.

2 Knit 2 stitches together and transfer them to the right-hand needle.

3 Two stitches are reduced to 1 stitch and the knitted garment slants to the right for an easy decrease.

Binding Off

To prevent your knitwear from unwinding, you must bind off. This technique holds the stitches together, and guarantees a beautiful finished edge. The abbreviation for binding off is BO.

1 Knit 2 stitches, as usual.

2 With the left-hand needle, lift the first stitch up over the second stitch and completely off the right-hand needle.

3 Knit the next stitch and repeat the second step until 1 stitch remains on the left-hand needle. Lift the final stitch off the left-hand needle and cut the yarn leaving a 6-inch tail. To complete the bind off, pull the tail through the last stitch and tie securely.

Abbreviations

Since U R a new knitter, we've made the patterns in this book easier to follow by not including abbreviations. Below is a list of common knitting terms. Remember to read each pattern completely before you begin knitting.

BO—bind off

CO—cast on

col—color

dec—decrease

Garter st—knit or purl every row

inc—increase

" or in—inch

K—knit

k2tog—knit 2 stitches together (right-slanting decrease)

LH—left-hand

P—purl

patt—pattern

pm—place ring marker

pwise—purlwise

p2tog—purl 2 stitches together

rep—repeat

rep from *—repeat instruction after *

RH—right-hand

rnd—round

RS—right side

sl st—slip stitch

st(s)—stitch(es)

St st—Stockinette stitch (knit 1 row, purl 1 row; repeat)

tog—together

work even—continue in pattern without increasing or decreasing

WS—wrong side

Gauge

The gauge gives you the number of stitches per width and the number of rows per length of your knitwear. Gauge in knitting is very important. To be sure your knitwear is the correct size, we suggest that you knit a 4-inch by 4-inch (10cm x 10cm) test swatch. If your test swatch is larger than the gauge in the pattern, change to a smaller needle. If your test swatch is smaller than the gauge in the pattern, change to a bigger needle. Gauge is the key to knitting clothes that fit properly. When you reach the correct gauge, you are ready to begin knitting a pattern.

Tension

Needle size, yarn content and how tightly or loosely you knit have a direct effect on the outfits you are knitting. If you are a tight knitter and produce more stitches per inch, use larger needles. If you are a loose knitter and produce fewer stitches per inch, try smaller needles. With practice, practice, and more practice, you will develop the skills to knit stylish clothes that look cool and fit great!

These two swatches were knit with the same needle size, same number of stitches, and same yarn by two different girls. You can see each knitter had a different tension. Before making each pattern knit a 4" x 4" (10cm x 10cm) sample swatch. If your swatch is smaller than the gauge, use larger needles, if your swatch is larger than the gauge, use smaller needles.

Materials

You will need the following materials and tools to begin a knitting project—Knitting Needles, Yarn, Scissors, and a Tape Measure or Ruler. Each pattern gives you needle size and yarn needed to knit the project. The additional materials below will make your knitting easier and fun.

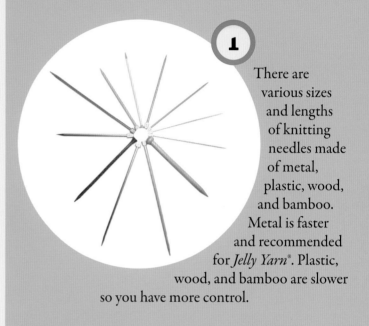

There are various sizes and lengths of knitting needles made of metal, plastic, wood, and bamboo. Metal is faster and recommended for *Jelly Yarn*®. Plastic, wood, and bamboo are slower so you have more control.

Stitch counters make it easier to keep track of the number of stitches you have made. Stitch markers help you see your stitches. Crochet hooks aid in getting dropped stitches and weaving loose ends, while the tapestry needle helps you sew it all together. Needle tip protectors helps prevent your knitting from falling off.

Stitch Patterns

Knit and Purl are the basic stitches for most knitting patterns. Once you learn these stitch patterns, you'll be ready to combine them and knit all the projects in this book.

Garter Stitch Pattern

With a Garter stitch pattern, you knit every row (page 13). This simple stitch is easy to recognize by its rows of bumps that look the same on the front and back.

Stockinette Stitch Pattern

With a Stockinette stitch pattern, you alternate knitting the first row (page 13) and purling the next row (page 13). The Stockinette pattern has v-shaped stitches on the right side, (the side worn on the outside) and bumpy shaped stitches on the wrong side (the side worn on the inside).

Ribbing Stitch Pattern

Ribbing stitch patterns are used to give a knitted garment an elastic edge for making waistbands, cuffs, and neckbands. For the double ribbing pattern in this book, cast on a multiple of 4 stitches, (4, 8, 12, 16, etc.). Knit 2 stitches (page 13), and then purl 2 stitches (page 13) across the row.

Needle Chart

Knitting needles range in sizes from 0 (2mm) to 50 (25.5mm) and come in 10 inch and 14 inch lengths. Small needles produce smaller stitches, while large needles produce larger stitches. To practice, use US #13 (9.00mm) needles and bulky yarn.

Needle Sizes

U.S.	Metric
0	2.00mm
1	2.25mm
2	2.75mm
3	3.25mm
4	3.50mm
5	3.75mm
6	4.00mm
7	4.50mm
8	5.00mm
9	5.50mm
10	6.00mm
10.5	6.50mm
11	8.00mm
13	9.00mm
15	10.00mm
17	12.75mm
18	14.00mm
19	15.00mm
35	19.00mm
50	25.50mm

Sewing It All Together

After completing your knitted pieces, you will have to sew them together. This requires practice and patience. We recommend using the Mattress stitch to join pieces that have an equal number of rows. This technique will produce an almost invisible looking seam.

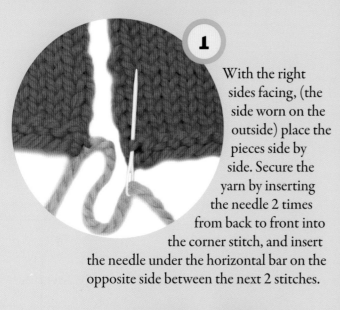

1 With the right sides facing, (the side worn on the outside) place the pieces side by side. Secure the yarn by inserting the needle 2 times from back to front into the corner stitch, and insert the needle under the horizontal bar on the opposite side between the next 2 stitches.

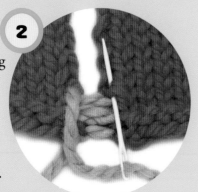

2 Continue inserting the needle below and above the horizontal bar on each side until the two pieces are completely joined.

3 Pull yarn ends to join seams and weave in loose ends.

Joining Yarns

Sooner or later you will need to add yarn or change colors. To avoid bulging and make it easier to weave in loose ends, join yarns at the end of a row.

Make a slipknot and draw the old yarn through, leaving a 6-inch tail. With the short tails in your left hand, slide the slipknot up to the needle and continue knitting.

Weaving Loose Ends

To prevent your knitted garment from separating during washing, weave in loose ends securely.

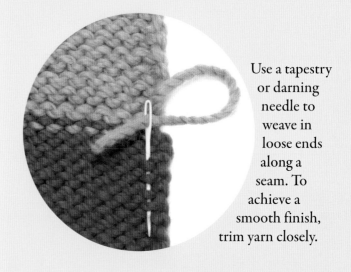

Use a tapestry or darning needle to weave in loose ends along a seam. To achieve a smooth finish, trim yarn closely.

How To Read a Knitting Pattern

Now that you can make a Knit and Purl stitch, you are ready to begin following a pattern. Patterns are written in shorthand to save space. We have included general abbreviations, terms, and symbols to help you understand a knitting pattern. Remember to always read instructions completely before beginning any knitting project.

Level
Beginner (knit and purl stitches are used)

Yarn (yarn label information)
For example: 2 balls Paton's Merino Wool 3.5 oz/100g, 120 yds (110m) Color: 233 Blush

Needles
Sizes #1 US (2.25mm) to size #50 US (25.50mm)
For example: #10 US (6.00mm) or size needed to obtain gauge.

Sizes (Multiple sizes are written in brackets)
For example: S (M, L, XL)

Gauge (number of stitches and rows)
For Example: In Garter stitch pattern, 24 stitches and 18 rows = 4"
*Asterisks/Brackets (number of repetitions)
For example: *K4, P8, K4 repeat from * 2 times.
Meaning: Knit 4 stitches, purl 8 stitches, knit 4 stitches a total of 3 times, or K4, P8, K4 3 times.

Parentheses (gives size, number of stitches, or length in inches)
For example: Sizes: 2 (4, 6, 8), Stitches: 16 (20, 24, 28), Inches: 8 (10, 14, 18)" Dimensions are given from smallest to largest.

Are you ready to read this pattern?
With #8 US needles and Lion Brand Yarn *Fun Fur* yarn, Cast on (CO) 16 (18, 20, 22) stitches. Work in Garter stitch pattern for 6 rows. Change to #10 US needles and Crystal Palace Yarns *Tingle* yarn.

Work in Stockinette stitch pattern until piece measures 8 (10, 12, 12)". Last row: *K2, P4, K2 repeat from * 5 times. Bind off (BO) loosely.

Blocking

Blocking your knitwear is quick and easy to do and prevents your knitted ends from curling or shrinking. Wool and cotton yarns are best for wet-spray blocking. Never block knitting with fuzz or fur novelty yarns.

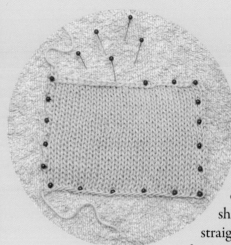

Before sewing together, pin the knitted pieces with rustproof pins to a blocking board in the desired size and shape. Be sure to straighten all stitches and rows. If you can't find a blocking board, don't worry. Just pin the garment, wrong side up, to a bath towel or ironing board. Use a plastic spray bottle to dampen the knitwear and pat with your hand to help the water soak into the fabric. When the knitwear is completely dry, remove the pins and blocking will be complete.

2 all about novelty yarns

Fuzzy Eyelash and shaggy Fur yarns are the rage! It's so easy to knit scarves, cuffs, and stuff with these favorite fun yarns.

Jelly Yarn

One of the hottest yarns! Knit glossy textures that are slick and colorful named after candy and ice cream flavors. How cool is that!

They are warm, wild, and crazy! Chunky & Funky yarns range from wool to chenille and spiky to funky. What's your mood?

Multi-strand Yarn

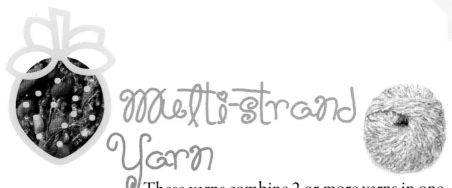

These yarns combine 2 or more yarns in one twisted strand and save you money rather than buying individual yarns. That makes cents!

Flat Yarn

Ladder yarn are very delicate while Flag yarns are colorful and puffy. Ribbon yarns are sooo silky. Create hip textures with Flat yarns.

Knitting Tricks & Tips

Sometimes the knitting needles just won't behave... Help is on the way! Look for advise and learn new knitting secrets.

Novelty Yarns

Knitting with novelty yarns is fun! There are many different types of yarn. In this book we feature five different yarns: Eyelash and Fur, Chunky and Funky, Multi-strand, Flat, and Jelly Yarn®.

With many projects, we combine yarns to make beautiful textures that look like difficult stitch patterns but are actually simple Garter or Stockinette patterns.

Each yarn is represented by a different, fun symbol on each project page.

 Ladybug = Eyelash & Fur Yarns

 Jellyfish = Jelly Yarns®

 Turtle = Chunky & Funky Yarns

 **Strawberry = Multi-strand Yarns**

 Cupcake = Flat Yarns

Eyelash and Fur

Eyelash and Fur are the most popular novelty yarns. You can knit the Boa Scarf, Cool Cuffs, Jazzy Denim Stripe, Bell Sleeved Sweater, and other fun embellished edges with these furry yarns. Eyelash has three or more super-thin fibers evenly spaced along a core center thread. Knit it with other yarns to create a light

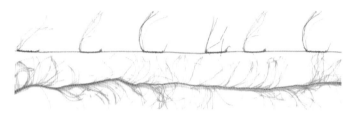

fringy edge. Fur yarns are straight, lightweight fibers on a core thread. Knitting with Fur yarn produces a shaggy texture resembling a plush stuffed animal. These yarns may be hard to see, but are very forgiving and won't show knitting mistakes!

Jelly Yarns®

Jelly Yarn® is the newest and coolest yarn in knitting. This vinyl yarn is available in Fine and Bulky weights, and comes in 7 yummy colors: Black Licorice, Blue Taffy, Pink Parfait, Raspberry Sorbet, Lemon-Lime Ice, Hot Pink Candy, and Orange Sherbet. You can knit the Jelly Bracelets, Jelly Purses, Beaded

Belt, and Beaded Flip-flops, with *Jelly Yarns®*. The knitted texture is slick and glossy. Knit with metal needles and dab the needles with silicone or ArmorAll® for an easy glide

Chunky & Funky Yarns

Chunky and Funky are perfect yarns for girls because they are soft, warm, and cuddly. These colorful yarns include, chenille, bouclé, slubbed, bulky wool

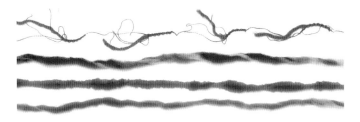

blends, and yarns with funky tufts of fiber. They are super-quick to knit and produce thick stitches that are very easy to see. You can knit the Choker, Pocket Pals, Mini Poncho, and Hip Skirt with Chunky and Funky yarns.

Multi-strand Yarns

Multi-strand yarns are a combination of two or more novelty yarn strands twisted together. For example: the Multi-strand *Combolo* yarn for the Boat Neck Top (page 68) is knit from Chunky & Funky, Flat Flag, and Ribbon yarns twisted together. And, the

Montage yarn for Tankini (page 80) is actually a combination of Flat Ladder and Chunky & Funky yarns together. These yarns can save you money because you don't have to buy each yarn individually.

Flat Yarns

There are 3 different kinds of Flat yarns: Ladder, Flag, and Ribbon. Ladder or railroad yarns have two thin parallel strands of thread joined by perpendicular crossbar fibers. This yarn is used in the Tankini Top.

In Flag yarns, there are many evenly spaced tufts of fiber along a center core strand. Colorful puffs dot the yarn for a hip texture. You can knit the Ruffle Shrug with Flag yarn.

Ribbon yarns, are silky slim flat bands of yarn. Some Ribbon yarns have feathery soft edges for a super-soft texture. You can knit the Denim Jacket Cuffs and Knitted Sleeves with Ribbon yarn.

Flat yarns work very well alone or combined with other novelty yarns for cool textures and colors.

Knitting Tricks & Tips

Knitting Tricks

Comb Your Fur Knitting

After knitting each row with Fur or Eyelash yarns, gently tug on long fibers to straighten them. With a fine toothed comb or fingernail, gently scrape on the needle after each new completed row. This will create a lush fur effect.

Gently comb the stitches on the needle after each row.

This is a completed sample of knitting showing how combing after each row produces a thick shaggy fur.

Knitting Tricks

Keep Track of Your Knitting With Stitch Markers

Some yarn is hard to see on the needles. When working with 2 or more strands on the needle it may be impossible to keep track of the stitches. When casting on, slip a stitch marker on the needle between each stitch. As you knit each stitch slip the stitch marker onto the right-hand needle each time. This will help keep an accurate stitch count. In addition, for better visibility, use color-contrasting needles.

Slip a color contrasting stitch marker onto the needle after each cast on stitch.

Slip a stitch marker onto the right-hand needle after each stitch.

Knitting Tips

Dropped Stitches

If you have accidentally dropped a stitch while knitting, don't worry. Mistakes happen and sometimes a stitch will slip off the end of your needle before being worked. A dropped stitch that has fallen several rows should be picked up as soon as possible. Here's how to do it.

Insert a crochet hook through the dropped stitch, hook the horizontal strand above the loop, and pull the horizontal strand through the dropped stitch. Repeat until you reach the top strand.

Then, slip the stitch onto the left needle from front to back.

NOTE: In Garter stitch, you will need to turn the garment over after working each strand.

Knitting Tips

Your Knitting Keeps Getting Wider

Did you ever find that your knitting keeps getting wider and wider? This often happens when you knit with more than one strand of yarn or if you use a yarn that splits easily. When you insert the right-hand needle into the left-hand needle stitch make sure you do not split the strand.

This is the WRONG way to knit. You are splitting the yarn and creating more stitches.

This is the CORRECT way to knit. Insert the needle from front to back under the entire yarn strand.

3 FUN STUFF & EMBELLISHMENTS

Boa Scarf

Funky red or bright orange boas are a quick-knit. Fur yarns keep you feeling oh-so warm and looking oh-so cool.

Jelly Bracelets

Easy slip-on-and-off bracelets knit with delicious blue taffy and lemon-lime ice *Jelly Yarn*® are a hot accessory with a jeweled heart. Sooo fashionable!

Jelly Purses

Be a style-savvy smartie with knit purses in cool raspberry sorbet and lemon-lime ice *Jelly Yarn®* to match your purse-onality.

Cool Cuffs

Accent denim jackets and sweaters with sassy ribbon or fur novelty yarns. Easy patterns are super-fun to make and chic to wear.

Jazzy Denim

Have fun dressing up denim skirts and jeans with knitted pockets, fur strips, and cool patches for that here-I-am look.

Knitted Sleeves

Turn a dull sweater into an exciting outfit with funky novelty yarns. Use your fave yarns to put together colors, textures, and looks.

Boa Scarf

Chloé looks cool wearing a cuddly boa scarf knit from two soft fur yarns that create a feathery texture. To make this super-easy scarf, use the Knit stitch on large needles. Stitch markers help you keep track of every stitch with the furry yarn. Mix and match fur colors for every season.

Yarn

1 (2) balls Lion Brand Yarn *Fun Fur* • 60yds (55m) / 40g (100% polyester) Color: #133 Tangerine

1 (2) balls Crystal Palace Yarns *Splash* • 94yds (87m) / 100g (100% polyester) Color: #9216 Orangeade

Needles etc

One pair US #13 (9mm) needles or size needed to obtain gauge.

Dimensions & Size

Short (Long) Instructions are for smallest size, with changes for other sizes in parentheses.

Measures 2.5" (6cm) wide x 30 (60)"/76 (152)cm long.

Gauge

In Garter stitch pattern, 11 stitches and 10 rows = 4" (10cm) with 2 strand of *Fun Fur* and 1 strand of *Splash* held together.

Garter Stitch Pattern

Knit every row.

Knit Stitch

Page 13

Substitution Yarns

Crystal Palace Yarns *Splash* = Bernat *Boa* Color: #81605 Tweety Bird or #81425 Flamingo

Lion Brand Yarn *Fun Fur* = Crystal Palace Yarns *Tingle* Color: #3866 Sunset Tweed

Boa Scarf Pattern

Body *(one piece)*

With 2 strands of *Fun Fur* and 1 strand of *Splash* held together, cast on 1 stitch and slide a large stitch marker on the needle.

Repeat 6 more cast on stitches and slide on 5 stitch markers between each cast on stitch for a total of 7 cast on stitches and 6 markers.

Work in the Garter stitch pattern, (Knit every row, page 13). After each stitch, slide stitch marker ring on to the right-hand needle. Knit for 30 (60)"/76 (152)cm or your favorite length.

Bind off loosely.

Comb fibers (Knitting Tricks & Tips, page 24) on needle after each row.

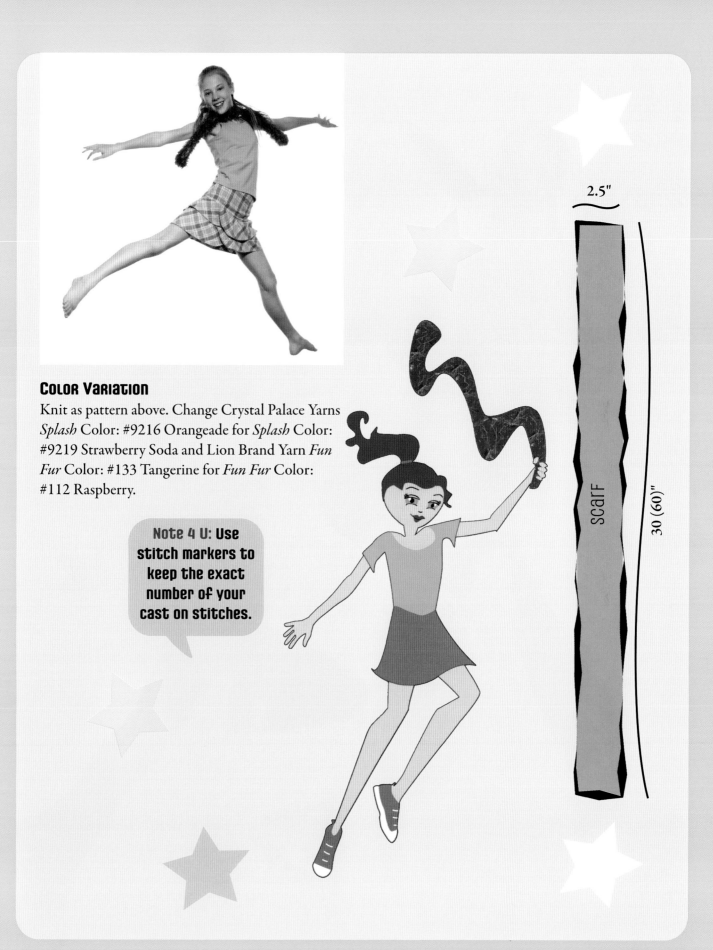

Color Variation

Knit as pattern above. Change Crystal Palace Yarns *Splash* Color: #9216 Orangeade for *Splash* Color: #9219 Strawberry Soda and Lion Brand Yarn *Fun Fur* Color: #133 Tangerine for *Fun Fur* Color: #112 Raspberry.

Note 4 U: Use stitch markers to keep the exact number of your cast on stitches.

2.5"

scarf

30 (60)"

Jelly Bracelet

New Jelly Bracelets are all the rage and fun to knit! Your needles will glide with blue taffy and lemon-lime ice Jelly Yarn®. Dress up your wrist for a casual or party look, like Hannah and Chloé. Super-easy and super-quick to make with Easy and Beginner pattern variations. Mix and match cool jelly colors with different glittering jeweled buckle hearts.

Yarn

1 ball Yummy Yarns® Fine *Jelly Yarn®* • 85yds (78m) / 200g (100% vinyl) Color: Blue Taffy or Lemon-Lime Ice

Needles etc

US #8 (5mm) METAL needles or size needed to obtain gauge.
Prym Dritz heart jeweled buckle Color: Lt. Pink or Lt. Green.

Dimensions & Size

Measures 1.5" (4cm) wide x 6" (15cm) long.

Gauge

In Garter stitch pattern, 3 stitches and 7 rows = 1" (2.5cm) with 2 strands of *Jelly Yarn* held together.

Garter Stitch Pattern

Knit every row.

Knit Stitch

Page 13

Purl Stitch

Page 13

Substitution Yarns

Replace Yummy Yarns® Fine *Jelly Yarn*® Color: Blue Taffy with Colors: Hot Pink Candy, Raspberry Sorbet, Orange Sherbet or Pink Parfait

Jelly Bracelet Pattern
Easy Version

Bracelet Band (one piece)

Cast on 5 stitches. Using 2 strands from the tail end, tie a very tight knot after last cast on stitch.

Knit (Knit stitch, page 13) across each row for 6" (15cm) or desired length (circumference of wrist.) Jelly bracelet will stretch over hand to fit wrist. Bind off loosely.

Note 4 U: Pull yarn strands from the center and outside of the ball at the same time.

Note 4 U: Wipe ArmorAll® along stitches on metal needles for easy glide.

Attaching the Buckle

Remove tong from buckle with pliers. Slide *Jelly Yarn*® knit band through buckle. Sew seams using *Jelly Yarn*®. Tie a secure knot with *Jelly Yarn*® by pulling strands until they stretch, then release.

Jelly Bracelet Pattern
Beginner Version

Bracelet Band (one piece)

This version creates a "selvage" that has even decorative edges.

Cast on 5 stitches. Using 2 strands from the tail end, tie a very tight knot after last cast on stitch.

Row 1: Knit across.

Row 2: Knit across.

Row 3: Step 1: Bring yarn forward, and position needle under stitch as if to purl.

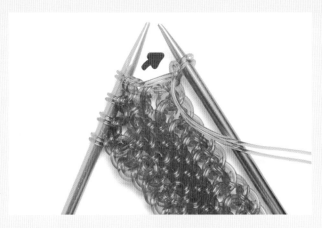

Row 3: Step 2: Then slip stitch onto right-hand needle.

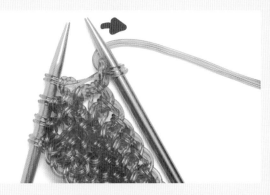

Row 3: Step 3: Bring yarn back, and position needle into stitch on left-hand needle in knit position and knit across remaining 4 stitches.

Repeat Row 3 for 6" (15cm) or desired length (circumference of wrist.)

Jelly bracelet will stretch over hand to fit wrist.

Bind off loosely.

Attaching the Buckle

Remove tong from buckle with pliers. Slide *Jelly Yarn*® knit band through buckle. Sew seams using *Jelly Yarn*®. Tie a secure knot with *Jelly Yarn*® by pulling strands until they stretch, then release.

Color and Buckle Variations

Mix and match *Jelly Yarn*® colors with different jeweled buckle shapes.

Knit a bracelet with 2 different Fine *Jelly Yarn*® colors: Pink Parfait and Raspberry Sorbet with a blue heart jeweled buckle.

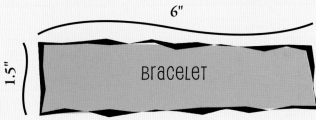

6"

1.5"

BRACELET

Jelly Purses

beginner!

Chloé and Hannah are carrying two fun styles of the Jelly Purse. These easy projects are created mostly in the Knit stitch. The purse with beaded handles is great for parties or special occasions with friends. The shoulder bag has a knit strap for a cool, casual look. Either way, they are a blast to knit with chic Lemon-Lime Ice *Jelly Yarn*®.

Yarn

2 balls Yummy Yarns Fine *Jelly Yarn*® • 85yds (78m) / 200g (100% vinyl) Color: Lemon-Lime Ice

Needles etc.

One pair each of US #10.5 (6.5mm) and US #8 (5mm) METAL needles or size needed to obtain gauge.

Prym Dritz Bag Boutique beaded purse handles Color: 9925.

Dimensions & Size

Measures 8" (20.5cm) wide x 6.5" (16.5cm) without strap.

Gauge

In Garter stitch pattern, 11 stitches and 60 rows = 4" (10cm) with 2 strands of *Jelly Yarn®* held together.

Garter Stitch Pattern

Knit every row.

Knit Stitch

Page 13

Purl Stitch

Page 13

Substitution Yarns

Replace Yummy Yarns® Fine *Jelly Yarn®* Color: Lemon-Lime Ice with Colors: Hot Pink Candy, Raspberry Sorbet, Orange Sherbet, Blue Taffy, or Pink Parfait

Jelly Purse with Beaded Handles Pattern

Front and Back *(one piece)*

Pull 2 yarn strands from the center of each *Jelly Yarn®* ball held together, cast on 23 stitches with US #10.5 needles. With 2 strands from the tail end, tie a very tight knot after last cast on stitch, leaving 15" (38cm) of cast on strands for sewing side seams later.

Rows 1–48: Knit across each row (Knit stitch, page 13).

Row 49: Purl across row (Purl stitch, page 13).

This will make a curve in your knitting to form the bottom of the purse.

Row 50: Knit across row.

Row 51: Purl across row.

Rows 52–99: Knit across each row.

Bind off loosely leaving a 7" (18cm) strand of yarn for sewing side seams later.

Finishing and Attaching the Beaded Handles

Lay the folded knitted piece on a flat surface and sew side seams together with 2 strands of Fine *Jelly Yarn®*.

With the beaded handle, clip the hook to each inside top edge of the right side of the purse. Repeat for left side.

Note 4 U: Wipe ArmorAll® along stitches on metal needles for easy glide.

Jelly Purse with Shoulder Strap Pattern

Front and Back *(make two pieces)*

Pull 2 yarn strands from the center of each *Jelly Yarn®* ball held together, cast on 23 stitches with US #10.5 needles. With 2 strands from the tail end, tie a very tight knot after last cast on stitch.

Rows 1–48: Knit across each row (Knit stitch, page 13).

Row 49: Purl across row (Purl stitch, page 13).

(This will make a curve in your knitting to form the bottom of the purse.)

Row 50: Knit across row.

Row 51: Purl across row.

Row 52: Knit across row.

Row 53: Purl across row.

Rows 54–99: Knit across each row.

Bind off loosely.

Shoulder Strap *(one piece)*

Pull 2 yarn strands from the center of each *Jelly Yarn®* ball held together, and cast on 6 stitches with US #8 needles. With 2 strands from the tail end, tie a very tight knot after last cast on stitch.

Knit across every row for 36" (91cm) or desired length.

Bind off loosely.

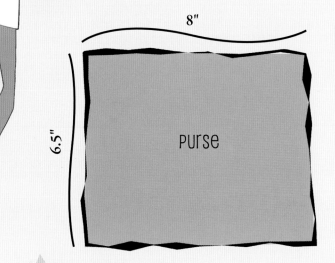

Finishing and Attaching the Shoulder Strap

Lay the folded knitted piece on a flat surface. Sew together, with 2 strands of Fine *Jelly Yarn®* using an overhand stitch and continue up the right side, sewing side seam and side of shoulder strap together. Repeat for the left side.

8"

6.5"

purse

COOL CUFFS

Create new fashions by embellishing a denim jacket or sweater with knitted cuffs! Olivia's slick sleeves are a chic way to make a one-of-a-kind design. The Sweater uses fur and mohair yarns for a casual cuff, and the Denim Jacket uses metallic ribbon yarn for a ruffle cuff. These cool creations are simple to knit.

easy! beginner!

Yarn

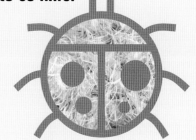

Denim Jacket Cuffs
1 ball Katia *Chic* • 70yds (65m) / 50g (54% wool, 43% nylon, 3% metallic polyester) Color: #5750

Sweater Cuffs
1 ball Lion Brand Yarn *Fun Fur Prints* • 57yds (53m) / 40g (100% polyester) Color: #211 Hawaii

1 ball Katia *Ingenua* • 153yds (141m) / 50g (78% mohair, 13% nylon, 9% wool) Color: #21

Needles etc.

On pair each of US #11 (8mm) and US #13 (9mm) needles or size needed to obtain gauge.

Denim jacket.

Sweater with long sleeves.

Dimensions & Size

Denim Jacket Cuffs • Measures 4" (10cm) wide x 13" (33cm) long.
Sweater Cuffs • Measures 2.25" (6cm) wide x 8" (20cm) long.

Gauge

Denim Jacket Cuffs

In Stockinette stitch pattern, 22 stitches and 20 rows = 4" (10cm) with US #11 needles and *Chic* yarn.

Sweater Cuffs

In Garter stitch pattern, 14 stitches and 20 rows = 4" (10cm) with US #11 needles and 2 strands of *Fun Fur Prints* and 1 strand of *Ingenua* held together.

Garter Stitch Pattern

Knit every row.

Stockinette Stitch Pattern

Row 1: Knit 1 row across.

Row 2: Purl 1 row across.

Repeat rows 1 and 2.

Knit Stitch

Page 13

Purl Stitch

Page 13

Easy Decrease

Page 14

Substitution Yarns

Katia *Chic* = Lion Brand Yarn *Incredible* Color: #209 Pastel Garden

Lion Brand Yarn *Fun Fur Prints* = Crystal Palace Yarns *Tingle* Color: #9016 Pink Carnation Tweed

Katia *Ingenua* = Plassard *Flore* Color: 077 Pink

Cool Cuffs Pattern
Easy version *(make two pieces)*

Cuff

With 2 strands of *Fun Fur* and 1 strand of *Ingenua* held together, cast on 8 stitches.

Work in the Garter stitch pattern, (Knit every row, page 13) for desired length to wrap around sleeve cuff edge or about 8" (20cm).

Straighten stitches on needle after each row. Bind off loosely.

Attaching the Cuffs

Place the knitted cuff on a flat surface. Lay the sweater sleeve on a flat surface and wrap the knit cuff around. Sew seams, (page 18) with 1 strand of *Fun Fur* yarn. Sew top and bottom of cuff to sweater with matching thread.

Denim Jacket Cuffs Pattern
Beginner version *(make two pieces)*

Ruffle Cuff

Using 1 strand of *Chic*, cast on 72 stitches.

Rows 1–2: Work in the Garter stitch pattern, (Knit every row, page 13).

Rows 3–8: Work in Stockinette stitch pattern, (Purl across row, Knit across row, page 13).

Change to #13 needles. Use the right-hand needle first. When all the stitches are on the #13 right-hand needle, put the needle in your left-hand, put the #11 needle away, and start using the other #13 needle.

Rows 9–11: Work in the Garter stitch pattern, for 4 rows.

Ruffle Row 12: Knit 2 stitches together, (Easy Decrease, page 14) across the row. Total stitches = 36

Row 13: Purl across row.

Row 14: Knit across row.

Row 15: Purl across row.

Row 16: Work in the Garter stitch pattern, for 5 rows. Bind off loosely.

Note 4 U: Use stitch markers to keep the exact number of your cast on stitches.

Attaching the Cuffs

Lay the knitted cuff on a flat surface. Fold in half and sew seams, (Mattress stitch, page 18) with 1 strand of *Chic* yarn.

Lay the jacket sleeve on a flat surface and insert knit cuff inside sleeve leaving a 2.5" (6cm) edge. Sew top of cuff to inside of jacket sleeve or adhere in place with fabric glue.

Tie a strand of *Chic* yarn around jacket cuff and button.

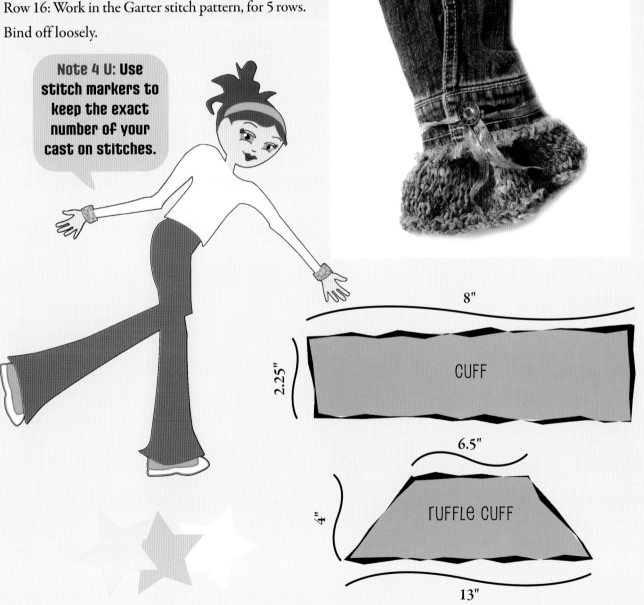

8"

2.25"

CUFF

6.5"

4"

ruffle cuff

13"

Jazzy Denim

easy! beginner!

Meghan shows three exciting new knit projects to jazz up your denim jeans and skirts. Knit hip little Pocket Pals with funky fur and chenille yarns. Create a Jean Stripe with micro-fur yarn. Then knit the Cool Patch, and rubberstamp for a personal look. So easy and so fun!

Yarn

Pocket Pals
1 ball Crystal Palace Yarns *Splash* • 94yds (87m) / 100g (100% polyester) Color: #7178 Cool Jazz

1 ball Caron *Glimmer* • 49yds (45m) / 50g (15% polyester, 85% acrylic) Color: #0008 Apple

Jazzy Jean Stripe
1 ball Crystal Palace Yarns *Splash* • 94yds (87m) / 100g (100% polyester) Color: #7178 Cool Jazz

Cool Patch
1 ball Lion Brand Yarn *Micro Spun* • 168yds (155m) / 70g (100% micro fiber acrylic) Color: #910 Lime

Needles etc

One pair each of US #10.5 (6.5mm), US #11 (8mm) and US #6 (4mm) needles or size needed to obtain gauge.

Denim jeans or skirt.

Invisible thread and needle.

Heart or flower rubber stamp and black permanent ink pad.

Dimensions & Size

Pocket Pals • Measures 4.75" (12cm) wide x 4.75" (12cm) long.

Jazzy Jean Stripe • Measures 1" (2.5cm) wide x 30 (32, 34, 36)"/76 (81, 86, 91)cm long.

Cool Patch • Measures 4" (10cm) wide x 3.25" (8cm) long.

Gauges

Pocket Pals

In Garter stitch pattern, 12 stitches and 22 rows = 4" (10cm) with US #10.5 needles and *Glimmer*.

Jazzy Jean Stripe

In Garter stitch pattern, 3 stitches and 4 rows = 1" (2.5cm) with US #11 needles and 2 strands of *Splash* held together.

Cool Patch

In Stockinette stitch pattern, 26 stitches and 32 rows = 4" (10cm) with US #6 needles and *Micro Spun*.

Garter Stitch Pattern

Knit every row.

Stockinette Stitch Pattern

Row 1: Knit 1 row across.

Row 2: Purl 1 row across.

Repeat rows 1 and 2.

Knit Stitch

Page 13

Purl Stitch

Page 13

Substitution Yarns

Caron *Glimmer* = 1 ball Plymouth Yarn *Sinsation* Color: #3332

Crystal Palace Yarns *Splash* = Bernat *Boa* Color: #81206 Toucan

Lion Brand Yarn *Micro Spun* = King Tut *Cotton* Color: #31

Pocket Pals Pattern
Easy version *(make two pieces)*

Pocket

Using US #10.5 needles and *Glimmer*, cast on 14 stitches. Work in the Garter stitch pattern, (Knit every row, page 13) for 22 rows.

Join 2 strands of *Splash* to *Glimmer* yarn. Knit for 6 rows or desired length of pocket.

Bind off loosely.

Attaching the Pockets

Position on jean skirt or jeans over existing pockets. Starting in upper left corner, sew along left side, bottom, and right sides of pockets with invisible thread. Use an overhand stitch to sew top edge of knit pocket to jean pocket.

Note 4 U: Join 2 strands of *Splash* first, then cut *Glimmer* yarn.

Jazzy Jean Stripe Pattern
Easy version (make two pieces)

Stripe

Using US #11 needles and 2 strands of *Splash* held together, cast on 1 stitch and slide stitch marker onto the needle. Cast on 2nd stitch and slide 2nd stitch marker onto the needle. Cast on 3rd stitch.

Work in the Garter stitch pattern, (Knit every row, page 13) for 30 (32, 34, 36)"/76 (81, 86, 91)cm long or desired length.

Bind off loosely.

Attaching Knit Stripe to the Jeans

Position on side seam of jeans, from below belt loops to bottom edge of pants. Starting at the top, sew fur stripe to side seam with invisible thread. Repeat for other side of jeans.

Cool Patch Pattern
Beginner version (one piece)

Patch

Using US #6 needles and *Micro Spun*, cast on 26 stitches.

Work in the Garter stitch pattern, (Knit every row, page 13) for 3 rows.

Work in the Stockinette stitch pattern, (Purl across row, Knit across row, page 13) for 20 rows.

Work in the Garter stitch pattern, Knit every row, for 3 rows. Bind off loosely.

Rubberstamping the Patch

Ink rubberstamp and test stamp on a piece of paper. Re-ink rubberstamp, and stamp in center of knit patch.

Attaching Patch to the Jeans

Position on jeans and sew along outer edges with invisible thread.

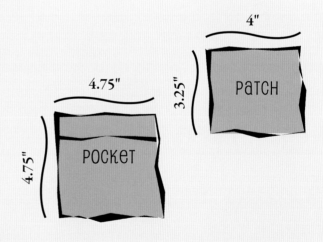

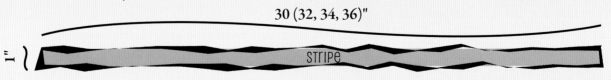

Knitted Sleeves

advanced beginner!

Give your sweaters some real pop! Olivia shows how much fun new knitted sleeves are to wear. Create sleeves with ribbon, fur, and fuzz yarns by knitting one row and purling one row. Knit each sleeve, stitch side seams, then slip over the arms of your sweater and sew together. Choose yarn colors to match your own sweater.

Yarn

1 ball Lion Brand Yarn *Micro Spun* • 168yds (155m) / 70g (100% microfiber acrylic) Color: #146 Fuchsia

1 ball Katia *Chic Print* • 70yds (65m) / 50g (54% wool, 43% nylon, 3% polyester) Color: #5750

1 ball Lion Brand Yarn *Fun Fur* • 60yds (55m) / 40g (100% polyester) Color: #112 Raspberry

1 ball On-Line *Punta* • 90yds (83m) / 50g (45% rayon, 45% nylon, 10% acrylic) Color: #36

Needles etc.

US #11 (8mm) needles or size needed to obtain gauge.

Dimensions & Size

S (M, L, XL) Instructions are for smallest size, with changes for other sizes in parentheses.

Total Sleeve Length: 14.5 (15, 15.5, 16)"/37 (38, 39, 40.5)cm

Gauge

In Stockinette stitch pattern, 13 stitches and 18 rows = 4" (10cm) with 1 strand of *Micro Spun* and *Chic* held together.

2 x 2 Ribbing Stitch Pattern

Row 1: (Knit 2 stitches, Purl 2 stitches), repeat across the row, ending with Purl 2.

Repeat row 1.

Stockinette Stitch Pattern

Row 1: Knit 1 row across.

Row 2: Purl 1 row across.

Repeat rows 1 and 2.

Knit Stitch

Page 13

Purl Stitch

Page 13

Easy Increase

Page 14

Substitution Yarns

Lion Brand Yarn *Micro Spun* = King Tut *Cotton* Color: #19

Katia *Chic Print* = Lion Brand Yarn *Incredible* Color: #209 Pastel Garden

Lion Brand Yarn *Fun Fur* = Crystal Palace Yarns *Tingle* Color: #9111

On-Line *Punta* = Ironstone Yarns *Little Loop* Mohair Color: #7

Knitted Sleeve Pattern
(make two pieces)

Sleeve

With 2 strands of *Micro Spun* held together, cast on 20 (24, 24, 28) stitches.

> **Note 4 U:** If Ribbing and Stockinette stitches are too difficult, work in the Garter stitch pattern, (Knit every row, page 13.)

Rows 1–5: (Knit 2, Purl 2) Repeat this Ribbing pattern until the end of the row.

Row 6: Join 1 strand of *Chic* and cut 1 strand of *Micro Spun*. Knit across row with 1 strand of *Chic* and 1 strand of *Micro Spun* held together.

Rows 7–15: Work in Stockinette stitch pattern, (Purl across row, Knit across row, page 13) for the next 9 rows.

Row 16: Drop 1 strand of *Chic* and add 1 strand of *Fun Fur*. Knit across row with 1 strand of *Fun Fur* and 1 strand of *Micro Spun* held together. Comb fibers (Knitting Tricks & Tips, page 24) on needle after each row.

Rows 17–21: Work in Stockinette stitch pattern for the next 5 rows.

Row 22: Drop 1 strand of *Fun Fur* and add 1 strand of *Punta*. Knit across row with 1 strand of *Punta* and 1 strand of *Micro Spun* held together.

Row 23: Purl across row.

Row 24: Knit 1. Increase 2 stitches, (page 14.) Knit across to last 3 stitches. Increase 2 stitches. Knit 1. Total of stitches = 24 (28, 28, 32) (Easy Increase, page 14)

Rows 25–29: Work in Stockinette stitch pattern for the next 5 rows.

Row 30: Drop 1 strand of *Punta* and add 1 strand of *Fun Fur*. Knit across row with 1 strand of *Fun Fur* and 1 strand of *Micro Spun* held together.

Row 31: Purl across row.

Row 32: Knit 1. Increase 2 stitches. Knit across to last 3 stitches. Increase 2 stitches. Knit 1. Total of stitches = 28 (32, 32, 36)

Rows 33–35: Work in Stockinette stitch pattern for the next 3 rows.

Row 36: Drop 1 strand of *Fun Fur* and add 1 strand of *Chic*. Knit across row with 1 strand of *Chic* and 1 strand of *Micro Spun* held together.

> **Note 4 U:**
> **Comb fibers, page 24, on needle after each *Fun Fur* row.**

Row 37: Purl across row.

Row 38: Knit 1. Increase 2 stitches. Knit across to last 3 stitches. Increase 2 stitches. Knit 1. Total of stitches = 32 (36, 36, 40)

Rows 39–45: Work in Stockinette stitch pattern for the next 7 rows.

Row 46: Drop 1 strand of *Chic* and add 1 strand of *Fun Fur*. Knit across row with 1 strand of *Fun Fur* and 1 strand of *Micro Spun* held together.

Row 47: Purl across row.

Row 48: Knit 1. Increase 2 stitches. Knit across to last 3 stitches. Increase 2 stitches. Knit 1. Total of stitches = 36 (40, 40, 44)

Rows 49–51: Work in Stockinette stitch pattern for the next 3 rows.

Row 52: Drop 1 strand of *Fun Fur* and add 1 strand of *Punta*. Knit across row with 1 strand of *Punta* and 1 strand of *Micro Spun* held together.

Row 53: Purl across row.

Row 54: Knit 1. Increase 2 stitches, Knit across to last 3 stitches. Increase 2 stitches. Knit 1. Total of stitches = 40 (44, 44, 48).

Rows 55–59: Work in Stockinette stitch pattern for the next 5 rows.

Row 60: Drop 1 strand of *Punta* and add 1 strand of *Fun Fur*. Knit across row with 1 strand of *Fun Fur* and 1 strand of *Micro Spun* held together.

Rows 61–65: Work in Stockinette stitch pattern for the next 5 rows.

While still on needle, lay knit sleeve over your sweater sleeve and make sure it is long enough. If not, knit 4 more rows in *Fun Fur* per inch of length needed until desired length.

Bind off very loosely.

Attaching the Sleeves

Lay the knitted sleeve on a flat surface and fold in half lengthwise. Sew seams, page 18, with 1 strand of *Micro Spun* yarn. Slip sleeve over your sweater sleeve and sew onto shoulder with *Fun Fur* yarn. Repeat for other sleeve.

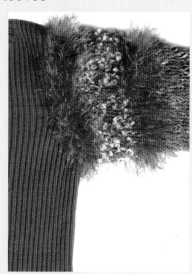

12 (13.5, 13.5, 14.5)"

sleeve

15"

6 (7, 7, 8.5)"

4 Beaded accessories

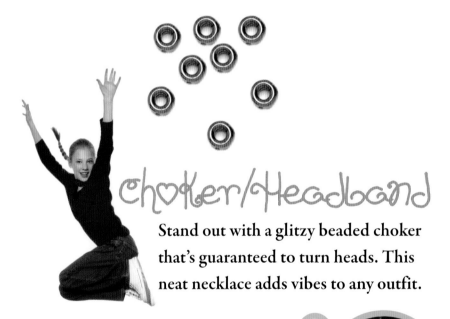

Choker/Headband

Stand out with a glitzy beaded choker that's guaranteed to turn heads. This neat necklace adds vibes to any outfit.

Beaded Belt

Jump on the latest trend with a hot belt knit with fine pink parfait *Jelly Yarn*®. Accent with glossy beads for a gotta-have fashion statement.

Beaded Flip-Flops

Go from the beach to the boardwalk with cool jelly flips. Match beads with your favorite outfit for that one-of-a-kind look.

Choker/Headband

easy!
easy!

Make your own knitted jewelry! Hannah is wearing a fab choker knit from soft chenille yarn. The choker pattern uses an easy knit stitch with metallic pony beads slipped between the stitches. This super-cool necklace also doubles as a headband. follow up with matching fun outfits and accessories. It's super-fast and super-simple.

Yarn

1 ball Plymouth Yarn *Sinsation* • 38yds (35m) / 50g (80% rayon, 20% wool) Color: #3369

Needles etc

US #10 (6mm) needles or size needed to obtain gauge.

16–(9mm) metallic pony beads.

Tapestry needle.

Dimensions & Size

S/M (L/XL) Instructions are for smallest size, with changes for other sizes in parentheses.

Choker • Measures 1.75" (4.5cm) wide x 9 (11)"/23 (28)cm long.

Gauge

In Garter stitch pattern,
16 stitches and 20 rows = 4"
(10cm).

Garter Stitch Pattern

Knit every row.

Knit Stitch

Page 13

Substitution Yarns

Plymouth Yarn *Sinsation* =
Lion Brand Yarn Chenille
Sensations Color: #136 Russet

Choker/Headband Pattern
(one piece)

Choker

Thread large tapestry needle and slip 16 pony
beads onto yarn.

Cast on 7 stitches, leaving 7" (18cm) tail for
tying the choker on your neck.

Knit across each row for 12 (17) rows.

Rows 13 or (18): Knit 3 stitches, slide 1 bead
on yarn and place bead behind needle and Knit
1 stitch, Knit 3 stitches.

Rows 14 or (19): Knit across row.

Rows 15 or (20): Knit 2 stitches, slide bead on
yarn and place bead behind needle and Knit 1
stitch, Knit 1 stitch, slide 1 bead on yarn and
place bead behind needle and Knit 1 stitch,
Knit 2 stitches.

Rows 16 or (21): Knit across row.

Rows 17 or (22): Knit 3 stitches, slide 1 bead
on yarn and place bead behind needle and Knit
1 stitch, Knit 3 stitches.

Rows 18 or (23): Knit across row.

Rows 19 or (24): Knit 2 stitches, slide bead on
yarn and place bead behind needle and Knit 1
stitch, Knit 1 stitch, slide 1 bead on yarn and
place bead behind needle and Knit 1 stitch,
Knit 2 stitches.

Rows 20 or (25): Knit across row.

Rows 21 or (26): Knit 3 stitches, slide 1 bead on yarn and place bead behind needle and Knit 1 stitch, Knit 3 stitches.

Rows 22 or (27): Knit across row.

Rows 23 or (28): Knit 2 stitches, slide bead on yarn and place bead behind needle and Knit 1 stitch, Knit 1 stitch, slide 1 bead on yarn and place bead behind needle and Knit 1 stitch, Knit 2 stitches.

Rows 24 or (29): Knit across row.

Rows 25 or (30): Knit 3 stitches, slide 1 bead on yarn and place bead behind needle and Knit 1 stitch, Knit 3 stitches.

Rows 26 or (31): Knit across row.

Rows 27 or (32): Knit 2 stitches, slide bead on yarn and place bead behind needle and Knit 1 stitch, Knit 1 stitch, slide 1 bead on yarn and place bead behind needle and Knit 1 stitch, Knit 2 stitches.

Rows 28 or (33): Knit across row.

Rows 29 or (34): Knit 3 stitches, slide 1 bead on yarn and place bead behind needle and Knit 1 stitch, Knit 3 stitches.

Rows 30 or (35): Knit across row.

Rows 31 or (36): Knit 2 stitches, slide bead on yarn and place bead behind needle and Knit 1 stitch, Knit 1 stitch, slide 1 bead on yarn and place bead behind needle and Knit 1 stitch, Knit 2 stitches.

Rows 32 or (37): Knit across row.

Rows 33 or (38): Knit 3 stitches, slide 1 bead on yarn and place bead behind needle and Knit 1 stitch, Knit 3 stitches.

Knit across each row for 12 (17) rows.

Bind off loosely leaving 7" (18cm) of yarn.

Attaching the Ties

Knot 7" (18cm) of yarn on each bind off and cast on end. Trim even.

Note 4 U: Make longer ties for a headband. Color match the beads to your clothes.

9"

1.75"

CHOKER/HEADBAND

Beaded Belt

beginner!

What could be more fun than a *Jelly Yarn®* beaded belt! Meghan looks hip wearing the belt over her top, or wearing it in her belt loops. Make this yummy pink parfait fine *Jelly Yarn®* belt knit with shiny glass beads in an easy Garter stitch pattern. Finish with a sparkly jeweled buckle.

Yarn

1 ball Yummy Yarns® Fine *Jelly Yarn®* • 85yds (78m) / 200g (100% vinyl) Color: Pink Parfait

Needles etc.

US #6 (4mm) METAL needles or size needed to obtain gauge.

150-200–Size E glass beads.

Prym Dritz oval jeweled buckle.

Invisible thread.

Dimensions & Size

S/M (L/XL) Instructions are for smallest size, with changes for other sizes in parentheses.

Measures 1.5" (4cm) wide x 26–30 (30–34)"/66–76 (76–86)cm long.

Jelly Yarn® is very flexible and can stretch up to 4" (10cm).

Gauge

In Garter stitch pattern, 4 stitches and 9 rows = 1" (2.5cm).

Garter Stitch Pattern

Knit every row.

Knit Stitch

Page 13

Easy Decrease

Page 14

Substitution Yarns

Replace Yummy Yarns® Fine *Jelly Yarn*® Color: Lemon-Lime Ice with Colors: Blue Taffy, Hot Pink Candy, or Black Licorice

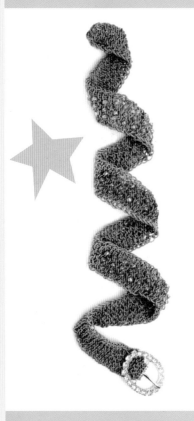

Beaded Belt Pattern *(one piece)*

Belt

String 150 (200) glass beads onto Fine *Jelly Yarn*®.

> **Note 4 U:**
> Wipe ArmorAll® along stitches on metal needles for easy glide.

Cast on 6 stitches.

Rows 1–21: Knit across each row.

Row 22: Knit 2 stitches, slide 1st bead up yarn strand and place bead behind needle and Knit 1 stitch, slide 2nd bead up yarn strand and place bead behind needle and Knit 1 stitch, slide 3rd bead up yarn strand and place bead behind needle and Knit 1 stitch. Knit 1 stitch. *(There should be 3 beads in the row.)*

Rows 23–25: Knit across each row.

Repeat rows 22–25 for a total of 23 (27)"/58 (68.5)cm or desired length.

Rows 26–46: Knit across each row.

Next Row: Knit 1. Knit 2 stitches together (Easy Decrease, page 14), Knit 2 stitches together. Knit 1. Total stitches = 4

Last Row: Knit 1. Knit 2 stitches together. Knit 1. Total stitches = 3

Bind off last 3 stitches.

Attaching the Buckle

Make sure the tong is centered on the right side of the buckle. With the tail end of the yarn, tie

the buckle bar to the cast on edge with a very tight double knot. Use a tapestry needle to sew the cast on edge to the buckle, wrapping around the bar each time. Sew equally on both sides of the centered tong.

COLOR AND BUCKLE VARIATIONS

Mix and match different *Jelly Yarn*® colors and different jeweled buckle shapes.

Knit a belt with Fine Blue Taffy *Jelly Yarn*® with a blue square jeweled buckle.

Knit a belt with Fine Black Licorice *Jelly Yarn*® with a pink heart shaped jeweled buckle.

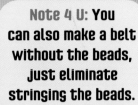

Note 4 U: You can also make a belt without the beads, just eliminate stringing the beads.

26–30 (30–34)"

1.5"

BELT

Beaded Flip-flops

beginner!

You'll flip over these beaded Flip-flops! Olivia is ready for the beach or boardwalk. Knit with super-cool Lemon-Lime Ice *Jelly Yarn®*, these mod flips are ultra-cute. For the bead row, just slip a bead between each knit stitch. Check out the removable version, mix and match beads and yarn colors to match your nail polish. How cool is that!

Yarn

1 ball Yummy Yarns® Fine *Jelly Yarn*® • 85yds (78m) / 200g (100% vinyl) Color: Lemon-Lime Ice

Needles etc.

US #5 (3.75mm) METAL needles or size needed to obtain gauge.

1 Pair of Flip-flops with plastic straps.

72-120–6mm A Touch of Glass cracked glass beads.

2 Silk Flowers.

1/2" Velcro® tape.

Dimensions & Size

S, (M, L, XL) Instructions are for smallest size, with changes for other sizes in parentheses.

Measures .75" (2cm) wide x 3.5 (4, 4.5, 5)"/ 9 (10, 11.5, 12.5)cm long.

Gauge

In Garter stitch pattern, 14 stitches and 32 rows = 4" (10cm) with 1 beaded strand of Fine *Jelly Yarn*®.

Garter Stitch Pattern

Knit every row.

Knit Stitch

Page 13

Substitution Yarn and Beads

Replace Yummy Yarns® Fine *Jelly Yarn*® Color: Lemon-Lime Ice with Color: Hot Pink Candy, Raspberry Sorbet, Orange Sherbet, Blue Taffy, or Pink Parfait

A Touch of Glass cracked beads = *Bead Solutions* Beads by the Box 6mm glass beads

Beaded Flip-Flops Pattern

Beaded Piece *(make two pieces)*

String 72 (90, 108, 120) glass beads onto Fine *Jelly Yarn*®.

Cast on 12 (14, 15, 17) stitches leaving 7" (18cm) strand of yarn for tying later.

Using the tail end and ball yarn, tie a very tight knot after last cast on stitch.

Row 1: Knit across the row (Knit stitch, page 13).

Bead Row 2: (Knit 1 stitch, slide first bead up yarn strand and place bead behind needle) repeat until there are 12 (14, 15, 17) beads in the row.

Row 3: Knit across the row.

Bead Row 4: (Knit 1 stitch, slide next bead up yarn strand and place bead behind needle) repeat until there are 12 (14, 15, 17) beads in the row.

Row 5: Knit across the row.

Bead Row 6: (Knit 1 stitch, slide next bead up yarn strand and place bead behind needle) repeat until there are 12 (14, 15, 17) beads in the row.

Row 7: Knit across the row.

Bind off loosely leaving 7" (18cm) strand of yarn for tying later.

Version 1

Attaching Permanent Beaded Piece to Flip-Flops

Note 4 U: Make sure bead hole is large enough to fit Fine *Jelly Yarn*® strand.

Straighten beaded knit piece. Use yarn tail and wrap around the entire length of the flip-flop strap, and tie knot securely underneath.

Glue silk flowers in center of each Flip-flop.

Version 2

Attaching Removable Beaded Piece to Flip-Flops

Use Velcro® tape to attach knitted piece to strap. Stick one piece of heavy duty Velcro® tape on top of flip-flop strap and the remaining tape on the bottom of the beaded knit strap and press together. Wrap yarn tails around both ends of strap and tie securely.

Glue silk flowers in center of each Flip-flop.

Note 4 U: Wipe ArmorAll® along stitches on metal needles for easy glide.

3.5 (4, 4.5, 5)"

.75"

BEADED FLIP-FLOP PIECE

5 FUNKY wardrobe

Boat Neck Top

Pony beads give this top plenty of pizzazz. Pair with your favorite jeans for a super-look. Sooo adorable!

Mini Poncho

Didja know, ponchos are hot! For extra pop, top off your look with side fringe and a large, round funky button.

Hip Skirt

Gurlz love to wear skirts 'cause they're always cool. This one features two sweetheart buttons for that soda-licious look.

Tankini Top

The tankini top is knit in yummy lime and pink yarns. Wear over a t-shirt for a layered look. Super-cool for school.

Bell Sleeved Top

Ruffle cap sleeves, edged with delicate rows of soft fur yarn, add style and flair to this easy-to-knit top, certain to dazzle your latest crush.

Ruffle Shrug

Kool kidz love fashions, and this apricot shrug tops the list. Ruffled cuffs and a tie front add lotsa extra style.

Boat Neck Top

easy!
easy!

Have fun knitting your first pullover with this easy Boat Neck Top. It's a simple project that's knit on big needles without decreasing or increasing. With this unique design, you knit two rectangles, sew side seams, and tie the top shoulders together with beaded strands of yarn forming the armholes. Wear it like Hannah in a funky-layered look.

Yarn

4, (4, 5, 5) balls Plymouth Yarn *Combolo* ● 47yds (43m) / 50g (66% nylon, 30% tactel, 4% polyester) Color: #1040

1 ball Lion Brand Yarn *Fun Fur* ● 60yds (55m) / 40g (100% polyester) Color: #112 Raspberry

Shoulder Ties (you can use any left over yarn)
1 ball Plymouth Yarn *Sinsation* ● 38yds (35m) / 50g (80% rayon, 20% wool) Color: #3369

Needles etc.

US #15 (10mm) needles or size needed to obtain gauge.

Size K crochet hook.

16–(9mm) Pony beads.

Tapestry needle.

Dimensions & Size

S (M, L, XL) *Instructions are for smallest size, with changes for other sizes in parentheses.*

Measures 36 (38, 40, 42)"/91 (96.5, 101.5, 106.5)cm wide x 10.5 (11, 11.5, 12"/26.5 (28, 29, 30.5)cm long.

Gauge

In Garter Stitch Pattern, 12 stitches and 18 rows = 4" (10cm).

Garter Stitch Pattern

Knit every row.

Knit Stitch

Page 13

Substitution Yarns

Plymouth Yarn *Combolo* = Moda Dea *Swirl* Color: 3962 Tinker

Lion Brand Yarn *Fun Fur* = Plymouth Yarn *Dazzlelash* Color: #101

Plymouth Yarn *Sinsation* = Lion Brand Yarn *Chenille Sensations* Color: #136 Russet

Boat Neck Top Pattern

Front and Back *(make two pieces)*

With 1 strand each of *Combolo* and *Fun Fur* held together, cast on 54 (57, 60, 63) stitches.

Work in the Garter stitch pattern (knit every row, page 13) for 3.5" (9cm).

Cut *Fun Fur* and continue in Garter stitch pattern for 10.5 (11, 11.5, 12)"/ 26.5 (28, 29, 30.5)cm or desired length.

Bind off loosely.

Finishing

Lay the knitted front and back pieces on a flat surface and sew side seams together, using the (Mattress stitch, page 18) with *Combolo* yarn.

Attaching the Shoulder

Cut 2–14" (35.5cm) strands of *Combolo*, *Fun Fur* and *Sinsation* yarns. Thread 8 pony beads on each *Sinsation* yarn strand. Tie a knot on each end and slide 4 beads to each end. Align 1 strand of each yarn side by side in two groups.

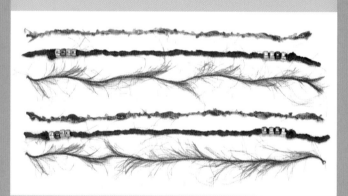

Lay the sewn top on a flat surface and insert a size K crochet hook through the two layers at the top shoulder edge 6.5 (7, 7.5, 8)"/16.5 (18, 19, 20)cm from the right side edge. Use the hook to pull the 1st group of strands through front and back

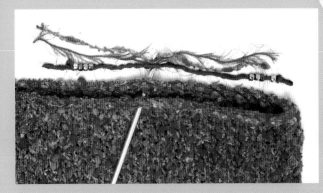

layers of the top. Pull halfway through and tie the strands together in a knot. Repeat for left side.

Note 4 U: You can put charms and other fun stuff on the strands.

Note 4 U: The top is going to look very wide because of the unique design, but don't worry!

36 (38, 40, 42)"

10.5 (11, 11.5, 12)"

FRONT AND BACK

Mini Poncho

easy! easy!

Ponchos are fun and Olivia is having a blast wearing this one in multi-colored wool blend yarn. Knit with big needles in the shape of a long rectangle, and then switch to smaller needles for super-easy shaping. To finish, fold to form the tube and collar, and then join seams with fringe. Guaranteed to be a hit this spring or fall!

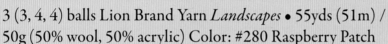

Yarn

3 (3, 4, 4) balls Lion Brand Yarn *Landscapes* • 55yds (51m) / 50g (50% wool, 50% acrylic) Color: #280 Raspberry Patch

Needles etc.

One pair each of US #19 (15mm) and US #35 (19mm) needles or size needed to obtain gauge.

1 Large button 1.5" (4cm) in diameter.

Dimensions & Size

S (M, L, XL) Instructions are for smallest size, with changes for other sizes in parentheses.

Chest: 28 (30, 31.5, 33)"/71 (76, 80, 84)cm

Length with collar folded: 10.5 (10.5, 11.5, 12.5)"/26.5 (26.5, 29, 32)cm

Gauge

In Garter stitch pattern,
7 stitches and 8 rows = 4"
(10cm) with #35 needles.

Garter Stitch Pattern

Knit every row.

Knit Stitch

Page 13

Substitution Yarns

Lion Brand Yarn *Landscapes* =
Rowan *Chunky Print* Color:
077 Girly Pink

Mini Poncho Pattern

Front and Back (*one piece*)

Using #35 needles, cast on 49 (52, 55, 58)
stitches.

Working in Garter stitch pattern, (Knit every
row, page 13) for 11 (11, 12, 13) rows. Use a
stitch counter to keep track of your rows.

Pull your knitting even to straighten out
stitches on the needle.

Change to #19 needles. Use the right-hand
needle first. When all the stitches are on the
#19 right-hand needle, put the needle in your
left-hand, put the #35 needle away, and start
using the other #19 needle. Knit every row, for
a total of 25 rows.

Bind off loosely.

Finishing and Folding the Collar

Lay the knitted poncho on a flat surface. Fold the top bind off edge over 2.5" (6cm). Then fold in half lengthwise. Angle the corner of the collar as shown. Sew the collar edge all the way around to the body of the poncho with the same yarn. Sew decorative button in angled corner.

Making and Attaching the Fringe

Place the folded poncho on a flat surface. Cut 20 pieces of 5" (12.5cm) long yarn for the fringe. Take 2 pieces of yarn and fold in half. Starting at the top, use a crochet hook to loop the end through both side edges of the poncho. Loop the 2 fringe strands evenly every other row down the side. Remember to loop through both side edges. Leave open 2" (5cm) from the bottom edge. Trim evenly.

Note 4 U:
It's easy to change needles!

28 (30, 31.5, 33)"

10.5 (10.5, 11.5, 12.5)"

FRONT / BACK

Hip Skirt

advanced beginner!

Chloé loves to wear this one-piece rectangle skirt knit with wool yarn on large needles. Start out with a bunch of cast on stitches, then, make an easy decrease to create the ruffle bottom. Knit an elastic waistband for a funky style. For school or a party, it's easy and pretty!

Yarn

2 (2, 3, 3) balls Lion Brand Yarn *Landscapes* • 55yds (51m) / 50g (50% wool, 50% acrylic) Color: #133 Pumpkin

1 ball Lion Brand Yarn *Wool-Ease Thick & Quick* • 153yds (141m) / 140g (80% acrylic, 20% wool) Color: #276 Summer Fields

Needles etc.

One pair each of US #15 (10mm) and US #17 (12.75mm) needles or size needed to obtain gauge.

1 yard–1/2" (1.25cm) flat elastic.

2 Heart buttons.

Dimensions & Size

S, (M, L, XL) Instructions are for smallest size, with changes for other sizes in parentheses.

Waist: 22 (24, 26, 28)"/56 (61, 66, 71)cm

Length with waistband folded 13" (33cm).

Gauge

In Stockinette stitch pattern, 9 stitches and 10 rows = 4" (10cm).

Stockinette Stitch Pattern

Row 1: Knit 1 row across.

Row 2: Purl 1 row across.

Repeat rows 1 and 2.

Knit Stitch

Page 13

Purl Stitch

Page 13

Easy Decrease

Page 14

Substitution Yarns

Lion Brand Yarn *Landscapes* = Rowan *Chunky Print* Color: 081 Shriek

Lion Brand Yarn *Wool-Ease Thick & Quick* = Rowan *Chunky Print* Color: 083 Corinthian

Hip Skirt Pattern *(one piece)*

Skirt

Beginning with 120 (130, 140, 148)"/304.5 (330, 355, 376)cm from the tail end of the yarn, cast on 116 (126, 136, 144) stitches with US #17 needles. Place a stitch marker every 10

Note 4 U: Measure 1" (2.5cm) of yarn per stitch of cast on yarn, plus 4" (10cm) extra.

stitches to help you keep track of your cast on stitches.

Row 1: Knit across row, removing the stitch markers.

Row 2: Knit across the row.

Rows 3–11: Begin with a Purl row and end with a Purl row. Work in Stockinette stitch pattern (Purl across row, Knit across row, page 13) for the next 9 rows.

Ruffle

Ruffle Row 12: Knit 2 stitches together (Easy Decrease, page 14) across the entire row. Total stitches = 58 (63, 68, 72)

Rows 13–19: Begin with a Purl row and end with a Purl row. Work in Stockinette stitch pattern for the next 7 rows.

Note 4 U: You can continue knitting additional Stockinette stitch pattern rows for a longer skirt.

Row 20: Knit 10 stitches. Knit 2 stitches together. Knit 10 stitches. Knit 2 stitches together. Knit 10 stitches. Knit 2 stitches together. Knit 10 stitches. Knit 2 stitches together. Knit the remaining stitches. Total stitches = 54 (59, 64, 68)

Rows 21–25: Begin with a Purl row and end with a Purl row. Work in Stockinette stitch pattern for the next 5 rows.

Row 26: Knit 10 stitches. Knit 2 stitches together. Knit 10 stitches. Knit 2 stitches together. Knit 10 stitches. Knit 2 stitches together. Knit 10 stitches. Knit 2 stitches together. Knit the remaining stitches. Total stitches = 50 (55, 60, 64)

Rows 27–31: Begin with a Purl row and end with a Purl row. Work in Stockinette stitch pattern for the next 5 rows.

Waistband

Row 32: Drop 1 strand of *Landscapes* and join 1 strand of *Wool-Ease*. Knit across row.

Rows 33–36: Knit across each row. Bind off very loosely.

Finishing and Making the Waistband

Lay the knit skirt on a flat surface, wrong side up. Place flat elastic band along the waistband and fold

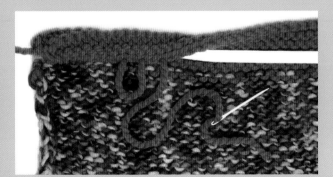

the bind off (top edge) in half. Let the elastic band hang over the sides of the skirt. Do not trim. Using *Wool-Ease* yarn sew the waistband over the elastic. Be careful not to sew into the elastic.

Fold skirt in half. Sew side seams, page 18, with 1 strand of *Landscapes* yarn. Do not sew waistband.

Stretch elastic 1" (2.5cm) from waistband and sew together with strong thread. Trim ends. Sew side seam of waistband with *Wool-Ease* yarn.

Position heart buttons in place on front side of skirt and sew with thread.

22 (24, 26, 28)"

2"

14"

SKIRT

Tankini Top

advanced beginner!

Meghan is wearing a cool tankini top knit with two brilliant yarns. Simply knit two pieces to make the front and back, add two straps to complete and you're ready for any get-together. The soft lime green and metallic pink yarns give this trendy top fire and sparkle. Show off this knitwear as a layered-look or wear as a tank.

Yarn

2 (2, 3, 3) balls Trendsetter Yarns *Montage* • 110yds (100m) / 50g (60% polyamide, 35% viscose, 5% polyester) Color: #1141

2 (2, 3, 3) balls Rowan *Calmer* • 175yds (161m) / 50g (75% cotton, 25% acrylic) Color: #483

Needles etc.

US #10.5 (6.5mm) needles or size needed to obtain gauge.

Dimensions & Size

S (M, L, XL) Instructions are for smallest size, with changes for other sizes in parentheses.

Chest: 27.5 (28.5, 29.5, 30.5)"/70 (72, 75, 77)cm

Length: 14.5 (15, 15.5, 16)"/37 (38, 39, 40.5)cm

Gauge

In Stockinette stitch pattern, 16 stitches and 20 rows = 4" (10cm) with 1 strand each *Calmer* and *Montage* yarn held together.

Seed Stitch Pattern

Row 1: (Knit 1 stitch, Purl 1 stitch) repeat pattern across the row, ending in Knit 1.

Repeat row 1.

Stockinette Stitch Pattern

Row 1: Knit 1 row across.

Row 2: Purl 1 row across.

Repeat rows 1 and 2.

Knit Stitch

Page 13

Purl Stitch

Page 13

Substitution Yarns

Trendsetter Yarns *Montage* = Plymouth Yarn *24K* Color: #1358

Rowan *Calmer* = GGH *Bali* Color: #18

Tankini Top Pattern

Front and Back *(make two pieces)*

With 2 strands of *Calmer* held together, cast on 55 (57, 59, 61) stitches.

Waistband Border

Border Rows 1–7: Knit 1 stitch, Purl 1 stitch (Knit stitch, Purl stitch, page 13). Repeat across row, ending in Knit 1.

Body

Cut 1 strand of *Calmer* and join 1 strand of *Montage* yarn held together. Work in Stockinette stitch pattern (Purl across row, Knit across row, page 13) until the top measures 8.5 (9, 9.5, 10)"/ 21.5 (23, 24, 25)cm *Make sure your last row is a Purl row.*

Neckline Border

Cut 1 strand of *Montage* and join a new strand of *Calmer* yarn. Make sure you have an odd number of stitches. If you do not have an odd number of stitches, Knit 2 stitches together, (Easy Decrease, page 14).

Next 6 Rows: With 2 strands of *Calmer* yarn held together, Knit 1, Purl 1, repeat across row, ending in Knit 1.

Bind off loosely.

Shoulder Straps *(two identical pieces)*

With 2 strands of *Calmer* held together, cast on 5 stitches.

Work in Stockinette stitch pattern until the strap measures 7.5 (8, 8.5, 9)"/19 (20, 22, 23)cm.

Make sure your last row is a Purl row.

Bind off loosely.

Finishing

Lay the knitted front and back pieces on a flat surface and sew side seams together (Mattress Stitch, page 18) with *Calmer* yarn.

Sew right shoulder strap to front and back, 3" (7.5cm) from edge. Repeat for left shoulder strap.

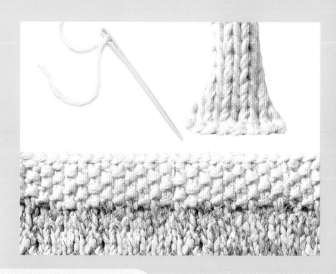

Note 4 U: If the border rows are too difficult, work in the Garter stitch pattern, (Knit every row, page 13).

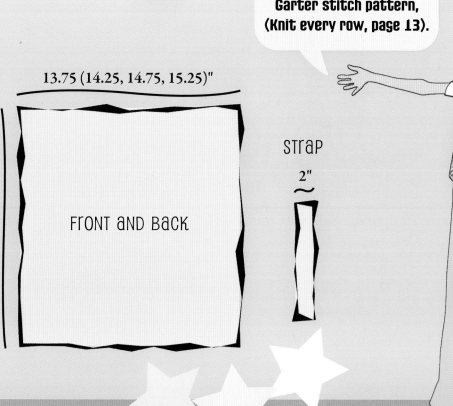

13.75 (14.25, 14.75, 15.25)"

14.5 (15, 15.5, 16)"

FRONT AND BACK

STRAP

2"

Bell Sleeved Sweater

advanced beginner!

Knit your first sweater! The fluffy ruffle-edged sleeves are too cute. Olivia is wearing this sweet sweater, knit in the Stockinette stitch, with a soft microsoft yarn. One-piece cap sleeves are easy to knit and sew together. Make a fashion statement; wear this hip top with jeans or a skirt. Either way, you'll treasure this adorable sweater.

Yarn

3 (3, 3, 4) balls Lion Brand Yarn *Micro Spun* • 168yds (154m) / 70g (100% microfiber acrylic) Color: #146 Fuchsia

1 (1, 1, 1) ball Trendsetter Yarns *Viola* • 187yds (172m) / 50g (100% nylon) Color: #5205

Needles etc.

One pair each of US #11 (8mm) and US #10 (6mm), 14" long needles or size needed to obtain gauge.

Dimensions & Size

S (M, L, XL) Instructions are for smallest size, with changes for other sizes in parentheses.

Chest: 28 (29, 30, 31)"/71 (73.5, 76, 78.5)cm

Length: 16 (17, 18, 19)"/40.5 (43, 45.5, 48)cm

Gauge

In Stockinette stitch pattern, 16 stitches and 20 rows = 4" (10cm) with 1 strand of *Micro Spun* yarn.

Stockinette Stitch Pattern

Row 1: Knit 1 row across.

Row 2: Purl 1 row across.

Repeat rows 1 and 2.

Knit Stitch

Page 13

Purl Stitch

Page 13

Easy Decrease

Page 14

Substitution Yarns

Lion Brand Yarn *Micro Spun* = Rowan *Wool Cotton* Color: #959 Bilberry Fool

Trendsetter Yarns *Viola* = Crystal Palace Yarns *Whisper* Color: #9305 Very Violet

Note 4 U: Straighten stitches on needle after cast on.

Bell Sleeved Sweater Pattern

Front and Back *(make two pieces)*

Ruffle Waist

Using #11 needles, cast on 112 (116, 120, 124) stitches with 1 strand of *Micro Spun* and 1 strand of *Viola* held together.

Comb fibers (Knitting Tricks & Tips, page 24) on needle after each row.

Row 1: Knit (Knit stitch, page 13) across the row.

Row 2: Cut 1 strand of *Viola* and Knit across the row with 1 strand of *Micro Spun* yarn.

Rows 3–8: Beginning with a Purl row, work in Stockinette stitch pattern (Purl across row, Knit across row, page 13.)

Row 9: Change to #10 needles, and Purl across row.

Row 10: (Knit 1 stitch, Knit 2 together, Knit 1 stitch) (Easy Decrease, page 14) across the row. Total Stitches = 84 (87, 90, 93)

Row 11: Purl across row.

Body

Row 12: (Knit 1 stitch, Knit 2 together) across the row. Total Stitches = 56 (58, 60, 62)

Next Rows: Beginning with a Purl row, continue working in Stockinette stitch pattern for 16 (17, 18, 19)"/40.5 (43, 45.5, 48)cm ending on a knit row.

Next Row: Purl 12 stitches, join 1 strand of *Viola* yarn and Purl 32 (34, 36, 38) stitches. Drop but do not cut *Viola* yarn strand and Purl remaining 12 stitches with 1 strand of *Micro Spun* yarn.

Next Row: Knit 12 stitches. Pick up 1 strand of *Viola* yarn again and Purl 32 (34, 36, 38) stitches. Drop but do not cut *Viola* yarn strand and Purl remaining 12 stitches with 1 strand of *Micro Spun* yarn.

Bind off loosely.

Sleeves (two identical pieces)
Ruffle
Using #11 needles, cast on 90 stitches with 1 strand of *Micro Spun* and 1 strand of *Viola* held together.

Row 1: Knit across the row.

Row 2: Cut 1 strand of *Viola* and Knit across the row with 1 strand of *Micro Spun* yarn.

Rows 3–8: Beginning with a Purl row, work in Stockinette stitch pattern.

Row 9: Change to #10 needles, and Purl across row.

Row 10: (Knit 1 stitch, Knit 2 together, Knit 1 stitch) across the row. Total Stitches = 60

Row 11: Purl across row.

Row 12: (Knit 1 stitch, Knit 2 together) across the row. Total Stitches = 40

Sleeve Bell
Next Rows: Beginning with a Purl row, continue working in Stockinette stitch pattern for 4" (10cm) ending on a knit row.

Bind off loosely.

Finishing and Assembling the Sleeves
Lay the knitted back and front pieces on a flat surface and sew shoulder seams together, (Mattress stitch, page 18) with *Micro Spun* yarn. Center sleeves and sew to side seams. Starting from the bottom, sew side seams leaving 7.5 (8, 8.5, 9)"/19 (20, 21.5, 22.5)cm.

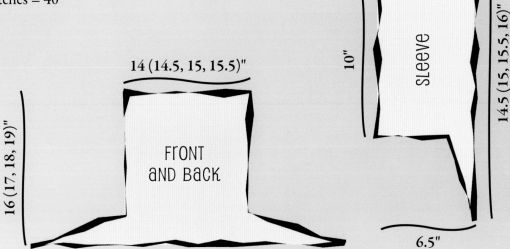

Ruffle Shrug

Meghan is wearing the latest in fashion knitwear, a cool Ruffle Shrug. This mini buttonless sweater is knit in four easy pieces with a simple Stockinette stitch in colorful novelty yarns. The waistband ties and cuffs are created in an easy Garter stitch ruffle. It's easier to make than you think. Now you can make your own cool shrug.

Yarn

2 (2, 2, 3) balls Lion Brand Yarn *Micro Spun* • 168yds (154m) / 70g (100% microfiber acrylic) Color: #186 Mango

2 (2, 2, 3) balls Crystal Palace Yarns *Little Flowers* • 145yds (134m) / 50g (66% rayon, 30% nylon, 4% metallic fiber) Color: #9555 Tulips

Needles etc.

US #10.5 (6.5mm), 14" long needles or size needed to obtain gauge.

Dimensions & Size

S (M, L, XL) Instructions are for smallest size, with changes for other sizes in parentheses.

Chest: 29 (30, 31, 32)"/73.5 (76, 79, 81)cm

Length: 10 (10, 10.5, 11)"/25 (25, 26.5, 28)cm

Gauge

In Stockinette stitch pattern, 16 stitches and 24 rows = 4" (10cm) with 1 strand each of *Micro Spun* and *Little Flowers* held together.

Garter Stitch Pattern

Knit every row.

Stockinette Stitch Pattern

Row 1: Knit 1 row across.

Row 2: Purl 1 row across.

Repeat rows 1 and 2.

Knit Stitch

Page 13

Purl Stitch

Page 13

Easy Increase

Page 14

Easy Decrease

Page 14

Substitution Yarns

Lion Brand Yarn *Micro Spun* = Rowan *Wool Cotton* Color: #962 Pumpkin

Crystal Palace Yarns *Little Flowers* = Knitting Fever *Spice* Color: #18

Ruffle Shrug Pattern

Back *(one piece)*

With 2 strands of *Micro Spun* held together, cast on 58 (60, 62, 64) stitches.

Border Rows 1–9: Knit every row, (Knit stitch, page 13.)

Next Row: Cut 1 strand of *Micro Spun* and join a new strand of *Little Flowers* yarn. Work in Stockinette stitch pattern (Purl across row, Knit across row, page 13) until the top measures 10 (10, 10.5, 11)"/25 (25, 26.5, 28)cm. Make sure your last row is a Purl row.

Bind off loosely.

Right Front *(one piece)*
Waistband and Ruffle Tie

With 2 strands of *Micro Spun* held together, cast on 105 (106, 107, 108) stitches. Place stitch marker at 29th (30th, 31st, 32nd) stitch.

Rows 1–6: Knit across each row.

Row 7: Knit 2 stitches together (Easy Decrease, page 14) for 76 stitches, Knit remaining 29 (30, 31, 32) stitches. Total Stitches = 67 (68, 69, 70)

Row 8: Knit across each row.

Row 9: Bind off first 38 stitches, remove stitch marker, and knit remaining 29 (30, 31, 32) stitches.

Row 10: Cut 1 strand of *Micro Spun* and join a new strand of *Little Flowers* yarn and Knit across the row.

Rows 11–15: Work in Stockinette stitch pattern. (Begin and end rows with a Purl row.)

Body

Row 16: (Right Side) Knit across the row to last 3 stitches, Knit 2 stitches together then Knit 1 stitch. Total Stitches = 28 (29, 30, 31)

Row 17: Purl across the row.

Row 18: Knit across the row.

Row 19: Purl across the row.

Repeat Rows 17–19: 10 (10, 11, 12) more times until there are 18 (19, 19, 19) stitches.

Bind off loosely.

Left Front *(one piece)*
Waistband and Ruffle Tie

With 2 strands of *Micro Spun* held together, cast on 105 (106, 107, 108) stitches. Place stitch marker at 29th (30th, 31st, 32nd) stitch.

Rows 1–6: Knit across each row.

Row 7: Knit 29 (30, 31, 32) stitches, Knit 2 stitches together for 76 stitches. Total Stitches = 67 (68, 69, 70)

Row 8: Knit across each row.

Row 9: Knit 29 (30, 31, 32) stitches remove stitch marker and bind off remaining 38 stitches.

Row 10: Cut 1 strand of *Micro Spun* and join a new strand of *Little Flowers* yarn and Purl across the row.

Rows 11–15: Work in Stockinette stitch pattern. Begin and end rows with a Knit row.

Body

Row 16: (Wrong Side) Purl across the row.

Row 17: Knit across the row to last 3 stitches, Knit 2 stitches together then Knit 1 stitch. Total Stitches = 24 (25, 26, 27) stitches.

Row 18: Knit across the row.

Row 19: Purl across the row.

Repeat Rows 17–19: 10 (10, 11, 12) more times until there are 18 (19, 19, 19) stitches.

Bind off loosely.

Sleeves *(make two pieces)*

With 2 strands of *Micro Spun* held together, cast on 120 (128, 136, 144) stitches.

Rows 1–6: Knit across each row.

Row 7: Knit 2 stitches together across the row. Total Stitches = 60 (64, 68, 72)

Row 8: Purl across the row.

Row 9: Knit 2 stitches together across the row. Total Stitches = 30 (32, 34, 36)

Row 10: Cut 1 strand of *Micro Spun* and join a new strand of *Little Flowers* yarn and Purl across the row.

Row 11: Knit across the row.

Rows 12–15: Work in Stockinette stitch pattern for 4 rows.

Row 16: Knit 1 stitch. Increase 1 stitch, (Easy Increase, page 14.) Knit across the row to the last 2 stitches then Increase 1 stitch. Knit 1 stitch. Total Stitches = 32 (34, 36, 38)

For Size Small continue working in the following pattern:

Rows 17–82: Work in Stockinette stitch pattern. At the same time you are working in Stockinette stitch, repeat row 16 increases on the following rows: 23, 29, 35, 41, 47, 53, 59, 65, 71, 77, 83 as follows: Knit 1 stitch. Increase 1 stitch. Knit across the row to the last 2 stitches then Increase 1 stitch. Knit 1 stitch. Total Stitches = 54.

Rows 84–87: Work in Stockinette stitch pattern beginning with a Purl row.

Bind off loosely.

For Size Medium continue working in the following pattern:

Rows 17–76: Work in Stockinette stitch pattern. At the same time you are working in Stockinette stitch, repeat row 16 increases on the following rows: 23, 29, 35, 41, 47, 53, 59, 65, 71, 77 as follows: Knit 1 stitch. Increase 1 stitch. Knit across the row to the last 2 stitches then Increase 1 stitch. Knit 1 stitch. Total Stitches = 54

Row 78: Purl across the row.

Row 79: Knit 1 stitch. Increase 1 stitch. Knit across the row to the last 2 stitches then Increase 1 stitch. Knit 1 stitch. Total Stitches = 56

Rows 80–90: Work in Stockinette stitch pattern beginning with a Purl row.

Bind off loosely.

For Size Large continue working in the following pattern:

Rows 17–88: Work in Stockinette stitch pattern. At the same time you are working in Stockinette stitch, repeat row 16 increases on the following rows: 23, 29, 35, 41, 47, 53, 59, 65, 71, 77, 83, 89 as follows: Knit 1 stitch. Increase 1 stitch. Knit across the row to the last 2 stitches then Increase 1 stitch. Knit 1 stitch. Total Stitches = 60

Rows 90–93: Work in Stockinette stitch pattern beginning with a Purl row.

Bind off loosely.

For Size X-Large continue working in the following pattern:

Rows 17–94: Work in Stockinette stitch pattern. At the same time you are working in Stockinette stitch, repeat row 16 increases on the following rows: 23, 29, 35, 41, 47, 53, 59, 65, 71, 77, 83, 89, 95 as follows: Knit 1 stitch. Increase 1 stitch. Knit across the row to the last 2 stitches then Increase 1 stitch. Knit 1 stitch. Total Stitches = 64

Row 96: Purl across the row.

Bind off loosely.

Note 4 U: Keep track of your cast on rows with a stitch counter or write them down.

Finishing and Assembling the Shrug

Lay the knitted back, right, left and front pieces on a flat surface and sew shoulder seams together, using the (Mattress Stitch, page 18) with *Micro Spun* yarn. Match up sleeves and sew to side seams. Sew sleeve seams.

BACK

10 (10, 10.5, 11)"

14.5 (15, 15.5, 16)"

13.5 (13.5, 14, 15)"

SLEEVE

14.5 (15, 15.5, 16)"

RIGHT FRONT

10 (10, 10.5, 11)"

7.25 (7.5, 7.75, 8)"

9.5"

LEFT FRONT

10 (10, 10.5, 11)"

7.25 (7.5, 7.75, 8)"

9.5"

Skill Level Project Guide

Easy

Projects for first time knitters, Knit Stitch only, Garter Stitch Pattern.

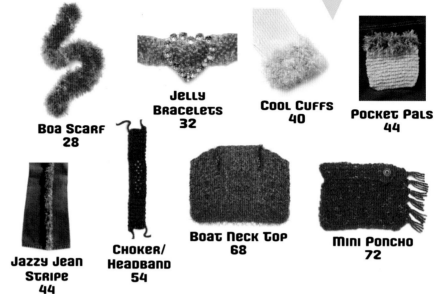

Boa Scarf
28

Jelly Bracelets
32

Cool Cuffs
40

Pocket Pals
44

Jazzy Jean Stripe
44

Choker/ Headband
54

Boat Neck Top
68

Mini Poncho
72

Beginner

Projects using Knit and/or Purl Stitches, Garter and Stockinette Stitch Patterns.

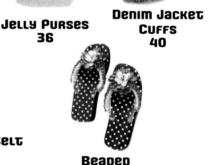

Jelly Bracelets
32

Jelly Purses
36

Denim Jacket Cuffs
40

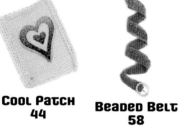

Cool Patch
44

Beaded Belt
58

Beaded Flip-Flops
62

Advanced Beginner

Projects using Knit and/or Purl Stitches, Garter, Stockinette and Ribbing Stitch Patterns, and Easy Increasing or Easy Decreasing for shaping.

Knitted Sleeves
48

Hip Skirt
76

Tankini Top
80

Bell Sleeved Sweater
84

Ruffle Shrug
88

Resources

These companies sell yarn to large stores.
Contact them for a store near you to purchase yarn.

Caron International
Washington, NC 27889
www.caron.com

*Crystal Palace Yarns
160 23rd Street
Richmond, CA 94804
tel: 510.237.9988
www.straw.com

Ironstone Yarns
P.O. Box 8
Las Vegas, NV 87701
tel: 800.343.4914
fax: 505.425.6967

Katia Yarn / Knitting Fever, Inc.
tel: 800.645.3457
www.knittingfever.com

Lion Brand Yarn
135 Kero Road
Carlstadt, NJ 07072
tel: 800.258.9276
www.lionbrand.com

Moda Dea
Coats Moda Dea
P.O. Box 12229
Greenville, SC 29612-0229
tel: 800.648.1479
www.modadea.com

Muench Yarns
1323 Scott Street
Petaluna, CA 94954
tel: 707.763.9377
www.muenchyarns.com

On-Line / Knitting Fever, Inc.
tel: 800.645.3457
www.knittingfever.com

Plassard Yarns
Distributed by Brookman Imports
105 Dixon Drive
Chestertown, MD 21620
tel: 866.341.9425
www.plassardyarnsusa.com

*Plymouth Yarn Company, Inc.
P.O. Box 28
Bristol, PA 19007
tel: 215.788.0459
www.plymouthyarn.com

Rowan Yarns
Westminster Fibers
4 Townsend W. Unit 8
Nashua, NH 03063
tel: 603.886.5041

*Trendsetter Yarns
16745 Saticoy Street / #101
Van Nuys, CA 91406
tel: 818.780.5497
www. trendsetteryarns.com

Yummy Yarns® *Jelly Yarn*®
362 Second Street Pike / #112
Southampton, PA 18966
tel: 215.953.1415
fax: 215.953.1697
www.jellyyarn.com
email: jellyyarn@3dimillus.com

* Yarn Contributors

Knitting Contributors
Lisa Gibson
Christen Parzych

Contact Information
Nick and Kathleen Greco
Dimensional Illustrators, Inc.
362 Second Street Pike / #112
Southampton, PA 18966
tel: 215.953.1415
fax: 215.953.1697

For Information on *Jelly Yarn*® visit
www.jellyyarn.com
email: jellyyarn@3dimillus.com

Knitting Websites
Basic Knitting Instructions
www.learntoknit.com

Craft Yarn Council of America
www.craftyarncouncil.com

Knitter's Review Forums
www.knittersreview.com

Knitting Techniques
www.dnt-inc.com/barhtmls/knittech.
html

Online Stitch Reference
www.stitchguide.com

The Knitting Guild Association
www.tkga.com

About the Authors

Nick and Kathleen Greco have co-authored several knitting books including *Yummy Yarns: Learn to Knit in 20 Easy Projects Featuring Fun Novelty Yarns*, *Yummy Yarns: Knits for Kids*, and their two newest books, *Girl's Guide to Fun & Funky Knitting* and *Beyond the Scarf*. Kathleen's knitwear designs have appeared on DIY's Knitty Gritty and in leading knitting magazines. Nick and Kathleen recently appeared on the popular NBC10! show in Philadelphia. Kathleen enjoys creating contemporary knitwear that is easy to knit and fashionably chic. The Greco's live and work in Bucks County, Pennsylvania

About the Photographer

Joe VanDeHatert, of Studio V Photography, is one of the most in-demand fashion and commercial photographers in his native town of Cincinnati. His photographs feature many of the area's top models. *Girl's Guide to Fun & Funky Knitting* and *Beyond the Scarf* are the latest knitting books featuring Joe's incomparable fashion savvy.

INDEX